Sweet & Easy Vegan

Sweet & Easy Vegan

TREATS MADE WITH WHOLE GRAINS AND NATURAL SWEETENERS

by ROBIN ASBELL

photographs by Joseph De Leo

CHRONICLE BOOKS

SAN FRANCISCO

Library of Congress Cataloging-in-Publication Data available.
ISBN 978-1-4521-0301-3

Manufactured in China

Design and typesetting by NOON SF
Prop styling by Shana Faust
Food styling by Cheryl Slocum
The photographer wishes to thank his crew
for their hard work, talents, and enthusiasm.

10 9 8 7 6 5 4 3 2 1

Chronicle Books LLC
680 Second Street
San Francisco, California 94107
www.chroniclebooks.com

ACKNOWLEDGMENTS

I dedicate this book to my late, great friend John Taylor, who encouraged me to write starting with my first article, years ago. He tasted my recipe tests for this book and gave me support and love to the end.

Of course, my sweetheart, Stan, my sister, Rachael, and my family and friends deserve my overflowing gratitude for helping me along the way. My agent, Jennifer Griffin, was there with great insight, hand-holding, and advice, even as she grew her family by one.

I owe great thanks to my diligent recipe testers: Melodie Bahan, Lisa Genis, Jill Jacoby, Marge Porter, Cathy O'Keefe, and Anita Bothun.

The talented people at Chronicle Books deserve much of the credit, with Amy Treadwell, Bill LeBlond, Doug Ogan, Tera Killip, and Alice Chau making sure that everything makes sense; Peter Perez and David Hawk shepherding my books into the bookstore; and a talented photographer giving the food the presence it has in the pages of the book.

Big hugs to the supportive friends who helped along the way: Fran Costigan, Linda Long, Jill O'Conner, and all my IACP colleagues who share so much.

Many thanks to all the wonderful people who read my work and come out to see me at classes and demonstrations. I couldn't do it without you!

CONTENTS

INTRODUCTION

Everybody loves sweets. Omnivores and vegans alike have a deep desire for the occasional treat, and why not? A cookie here and there adds joy to life, and if your diet is generally balanced, it really isn't a problem. Killjoys may recommend giving up eating sweet treats, but the fact is, most people like them: you like them, your family likes them, and they aren't going away anytime soon.

This book is my answer to the sweets craving, in which the sweets you eat are as nutritious and healthful as I can make them without sacrificing the pleasure of sweetness. I'm not claiming that eating these treats will make the pounds melt away; I'm simply trying to make sure that when you decide to eat a cookie or other sweets, they will be packed with real food, like whole grains, fruit, and nuts—and sweeteners in as unrefined and natural a state as possible. Junk food is just empty calories, but these calories are nutrient-dense. In fact, you may find that eating high-fiber, nutritious treats is so much more satisfying that you eat less of them as a result.

You don't have to adhere to any particular diet, vegan or otherwise, to enjoy these treats. I found that one of the great joys in developing the recipes for this book was sharing my treats with friends, neighbors, and coworkers who weren't particularly vegan or into whole grains. Their glowing and enthusiastic praise was encouraging. Beyond letting me know these recipes are truly tasty, the positive response proved beyond a shadow of a doubt

that people would come around once they actually got a bite. The proof is in the pudding—or the scone, cake, cookie, or biscuit, as the case may be.

CHOOSING SWEETNESS

For most bakers, the main sweeteners are white sugar and brown sugar (which is simply white sugar with some molasses mixed in). These sweeteners make life simple. Although they are familiar and therefore easy to cook with, they have some serious downsides. White sugar is made from sugarcane juice or sugar beets that have been refined to remove essentially all vitamin and mineral content, and the spritz of molasses that coats brown sugar contributes almost no nutrients. Whether in the form of refined sugar or high-fructose corn syrup, Americans eat an average of almost ½ cup/110 g of sugar per day and by some estimates the average person in the United Kingdom consumes his or her own weight in sugar each year—plus 20 lb/9 kg of corn syrup. That's an awful lot of calories to dedicate to something with no nutrients other than fast-burning carbohydrates.

Still, our desire for sweetness is a natural part of our physiology. In our not-so-distant hunter-gatherer past, sweetness was a signal that a fruit or vegetable was ripe and at its most nutritious. Finding a patch of ripe berries or a date palm dropping sugary fruit was a chance to get valuable nutrients that perhaps hadn't been available for a while. Sitting down to a feast and stuffing in as much as you could was a smart way to survive. Unfortunately, that drive has remained even as the world around us has become a twenty-four-hour buffet, too often filled with refined, processed, nutrient-poor foodstuffs. Instead of the scent of wild strawberries leading to a belly stuffed with nutritious fruit, rich in fiber, vitamins, and phytonutrients, a sniff of Cinnabon or a bag of Halloween candy can lead to a binge on sugary, high-fat foods.

It should come as no surprise that manufacturers know what you like and are happy to sell it to you. Sugar and high-fructose corn syrup are cheap and make junk food taste good. They hit your bloodstream with a surge of pure sugar, almost like a drug. For vegans, there's also the downside that in some cases the processing of refined cane sugar involves filtration through bone char. The Vegetarian Resource Group estimates that 20 percent of the white sugar sold in the United States is filtered this way. The best answer to your innate drive for sweets is to make your own treats using real, whole foods and sweeteners that are as close to their natural state as possible, which ensures that they deliver not just sweetness, but also superior nutrition.

REAPING THE REWARDS OF SUPERIOR NUTRITION

Before refined sweeteners became such a cheap, readily available source of sweetness, people found other ways to sweeten foods. Those less-refined sweeteners are less like drugs and more like food. They are wholesome and still contain many of the nutrients of the plants they were made from. A study published in the *Journal of the American Dietetic Association* in 2009 took a look at just one nutritional difference between sugar and alternative sweeteners: antioxidant content. The researchers found that there are no antioxidants in sugar or corn syrup, but varying degrees of antioxidant activity in natural sweeteners (other than agave syrup). Molasses, date sugar, brown rice syrup, and barley malt syrup had the highest antioxidant content, while maple syrup and rapadura cane sweeteners were just below them. The researchers concluded that replacing the average daily intake of refined sweeteners with antioxidant-rich alternative sweeteners could increase antioxidant consumption as much as eating a serving of blueberries or nuts.

Navinda Seeram, a plant scientist at the University of Rhode Island, has devoted a great deal of research to maple syrup. In 2011, he announced that he has identified fifty-four beneficial compounds in maple syrup, some with antioxidant and anti-inflammatory properties. The maple trees apparently produce these chemicals as part of their immune response to the wounds made to tap the syrup, and when we consume these compounds, they act to boost our immunity, as well. In addition, maple syrup is high in the minerals manganese and zinc, which also function as antioxidants and are crucial for many processes in the body.

The terms "evaporated cane juice" and "dehydrated cane juice" may be applied to a broad range of alternative sweeteners. All have the advantage that you can substitute them, in an equal ratio, for white or brown sugar. Some are made by fully refining sugarcane juice and then adding back in a bit of the molasses removed during the refining process. These sugars are shiny and crystalline, a sure sign that they are heavily processed. Other cane sugar products are superior, particularly rapadura, a type of sugar made by drying sugarcane juice, so it still contains most of the original molasses content, along with its minerals and antioxidants. Sucanat is a brand name for this type of sugar. I suggest that you choose Sucanat or rapadura—just be aware that these sugars have a stronger flavor. They also don't melt the way that refined sugars do, but they do bring distinctive and delicious sugarcane flavor to sweet treats.

CONSIDERATIONS WHEN SUBSTITUTING ALTERNATIVE SWEETENERS

Beyond having slightly more assertive flavors, alternative sweeteners bring other qualities to baked goods, and sometimes recipes must be adjusted. Dry sweeteners like Sucanat, granular palm sugar, and evaporated cane juice work most like granular sugars. If you aren't strict about avoiding refined sugar, you can use brown sugar in recipes calling for Sucanat or palm sugar. Traditional palm sugar, sometimes called coconut sugar, is a grainy paste; it's typically available in Asian markets. It falls between dry and liquid sweeteners in terms of how it's used. Because it's such a wonderful food, I like to use it often. It's a little trickier to work with, as you have to chop, grate, or crush before use so that it can be mixed in. If that seems like a pain, use Sucanat. Palm sugar paste is easiest to use in dishes like puddings and sauces, where it's melted in a liquid.

I like to use liquid sweeteners like maple syrup, brown rice syrup, and agave syrup because they're generally less refined than other sweeteners and contain more nutrients. However, substituting them in recipes does require that you adjust the liquids, usually cutting them by approximately ¼ to ½ cup/60 to 120 ml per 1 cup/ 240 ml of liquid sweetener used. Many of the whole sweeteners, both liquid and dry forms, brown more quickly than white sugar, so it's important to bake at moderate temperatures.

Part of the beauty of working with natural products is their uniqueness. Each of the natural sweeteners used here has its own flavors, moisture content, and level of sweetness. For example, brown rice syrup is less sweet than an equal amount of refined sugar, whereas maple syrup and agave syrup are sweeter. On the other hand, the stronger flavor of maple syrup gives a baked good a very different character than the more neutral taste of agave. In this book, I have chosen the sweetener that gives the sweetness and flavor appropriate to each recipe.

THE BENEFITS OF COMBINING SWEETENERS WITH WHOLE FOODS

So we have these wonderful alternative sweeteners that contain many or all of the nutrients in the plants or plant products from which they're derived. They add good things to your diet, as well as sweetness. The next issue to consider is the effect that these sweeteners have on blood sugar. While this is a complicated phenomenon, a few simple things can help you to navigate the choices before you. First, you may be interested in the glycemic index. This scale, originally devised to help diabetics better understand the effects that food choices had on their health, rates how quickly the sugars from various foods enter the bloodstream. Basically, small amounts of single foods were fed to subjects, and their blood sugar levels were monitored for the following two hours. Anything under 56 is considered low. Refined sugar has a glycemic index of 64, whereas in almost all cases alternative sweeteners have lower values.

Nutrients in Various Sweeteners (mg/100g)

	Palm sugar	Agave syrup	Honey	Maple syrup	Brown sugar	Refined white sugar	Evaporated cane juice
Phosphorus	79	7	4	2	4	0	31.7
Potassium	1030	1	52	204	133	2.5	742
Calcium	8	1.5	6	67	83	6	108.9
Magnesium	29	1	2	14	9	1	8
Sodium	45	1	4	9	28	1	0.33
Chloride	470	0	0	0	16	10	0
Sulfer	26	0	0	0	13	2	0
Boron	0.6	0	0	0	0	0	0
Zinc	2	0.2	0.2	4.2	0	0.1	1.5
Manganese	0.1	0.1	0.1	3.3	0.1	0	0
Iron	2	1	0.4	1.2	1.7	0.1	4.29
Copper	0.23	0.1	0	0.1	0	0	0.2
Thiamin	0.41	0	0	0	0	0	13.8
Vitamin C	23.4	0.5	0.5	0	0	0	79

Sources: "Comparison of the Elemental Content of Three Sources of Edible Sugar." analyzed by PCA-TAL, Sept. 11, 2000 (MI Secretaria et al., 2003), in parts per million (ppm or mg/L): and nutrutiondata.com

In practice, though, we don't sit down to a spoonful of maple syrup. We eat our sweeteners in concert with other foods. And those other foods can have profound effects on blood sugar as well. Fiber and fat both have the effect of slowing the absorption of whatever sweetener you consume. That means that the combinations of whole grains, healthful fats, and whole fiber-rich nuts, seeds, and fruits that make up the treats in this book work to keep your blood sugar on an even keel, even while you are enjoying cookies and cake. In fact, if the recipes in this book motivate you to eat more whole grains, you will reap many benefits, beyond stable blood sugar.

WHY WHOLE GRAINS

It's hard to miss the messages recommending that you eat more whole grains. Bread and cereal commercials tout the whole-grain credentials of various breads, cereals, and other products. However, despite all the good reasons to eat whole grains, people have been hesitant to adopt them into their diets. Changing food habits is hard, and many people stick with refined products out of habit or because they're convinced that whole grains just don't taste as good.

HEALTH BENEFITS OF WHOLE GRAINS

Whether you are vegan or not, eating whole grains is really, really good for you. Study after study has found that consumption of these tiny powerhouses is akin to a magic bullet for good health. According to the Whole Grains Council, eating three servings of whole grains per day reduces risk of stroke by 30 to 36 percent, risk of type 2 diabetes by 21 to 30 percent, and risk of heart disease by 25 to 28 percent. People who eat whole grains have healthier blood pressure and carotid arteries, less gum disease and tooth loss, and lower risk of inflammatory disease, colorectal cancer, and asthma.

Consumption of whole grains is also linked to healthy body weight. The anticarbohydrate folks who say bread makes you fat aren't looking at the whole picture. Like white sugar, refined white flour is stripped of its natural nutrients. It also has a higher glycemic index than whole-wheat flour and delivers empty calories without the balancing fiber to slow its release into your bloodstream. This helps explain why those who eat more whole grains have lower concentrations of trunk fat, which fills in around your organs inside your body cavity—the kind of fat that's linked to diabetes and heart disease.

Remember that dietary fads and fashions come and go. Artificial sweeteners, low-carb diets, and fat-free products have all had their day in the sun—and all have failed to solve our obesity crisis, and have often created new problems. Your best bet is to hang on to the basics. We human beings evolved eating whole, unprocessed foods, and that's what our bodies digest and run best on, not food engineered in a lab. When confronted with the next food fad, ask yourself, "Is it a whole, natural food? Is it minimally processed and something that humans have eaten for thousands of years?" When it comes to whole grains, the answer is yes.

Whole grains are the solid foundation of a nourishing diet, but too many people cling to processed, refined foods. Hearty, chewy, filling whole-grain baked goods are a great way to tempt your family and friends to eat more healthful real food. The recommendation that we strive to eat three servings a day is based on the expectation that you will eat none. More is better, and if you eat almost exclusively whole-grain foods instead of white refined foods, you will significantly raise your intake of fiber, protein, trace minerals, and even antioxidants. Why eat stripped-down refined foods, when whole foods are so delicious?

Whole grains are also full of flavor. We may have adjusted to the neutral taste of white flour, and the pure hit of white sugar in our desserts, but we can learn to appreciate whole desserts, too.

Take a bite of whole-wheat bread. Chew it slowly, savoring the texture and flavor. Notice how, unlike white bread, it has nuttiness, subtle sweetness, and satisfying chewiness. It has some weight and presence, some gravitas. Like the ancient food that it is, it commands attention.

CONSIDERATIONS WHEN BAKING WITH WHOLE GRAINS

Both whole grains and alternative sweeteners bring more flavor to the table than their refined counterparts. In these recipes, a palette of colorful tastes are brought into each composition, balancing and complementing the base ingredients. With so much going on in the background flavors, a little more cinnamon, vanilla, or chocolate can help bring a familiar flavor to the foreground.

Whole-grain flours are weightier, being studded with bits of bran and germ, so more leavening may be required (or, in the case of yeasted doughs, more rising time).

And because whole flours contain the bran and germ, they have a lower ratio of gluten and starches to help hold structure in baked goods. If you aren't gluten intolerant, pure gluten flour is a handy way to add a little structure to your whole-grain baked goods, along with more chewiness and wheat flavor. A little goes a long way, so you need only add 1 tsp here and there.

In some of these recipes I include some unbleached flour to help create the expected texture, but the majority of the flour will be whole-grain. In these cases, feel free to experiment with using 100 percent whole-grain flour if you like.

Like all natural products, whole-grain flours may vary from brand to brand. The main difference you might find is that some whole-wheat flours are ground more or less coarsely. For most sweet treats, finely ground flours are the better choice, and a finely ground whole-wheat pastry flour is the workhorse in the sweet vegan kitchen. White whole-wheat flour may sound like some kind of marketing scheme, but don't be put off by the term "white." It's made from a variety of wheat that has an albino bran layer, making it paler in color than regular whole-wheat flour. The recipes in this book were all tested using Bob's Red Mill flours and oats, which are widely available.

Once you get away from supersweet sugars and grow accustomed to the presence of whole grains, your palate will adjust. In time you'll come to love this way of eating, especially because you'll know that the recipes you make with alternative sweeteners and whole-grain flours are so much more healthful than conventional recipes, not to

mention most premade, store-bought products. Even so, calories are calories, so you still need to eat these sweets in moderation. But you'll probably find that easier to do when you aren't on a roller coaster of blood sugar spikes.

VEGAN, THE WHY AND HOW

Given that you're holding this book in your hands, chances are you have some idea of what vegan means. Vegan baked goods are made with no eggs, dairy, or honey. For some vegans, that extends to avoiding sugars processed using bone char and embracing healthier alternative sweeteners. People come to a vegan diet for a variety of reasons. Some do so out of a concern for the welfare of animals. Some are concerned about the carbon footprint of their diet and their impact on the environment. Some do so for health reasons, in a desire to avoid saturated fat, cholesterol, and white sugar. For many people, it's a combination of all of the above and may change from day to day. But basically it boils down to eating a more plant-based diet.

Interest in this way of eating is growing, and as ever, plenty of enterprising businesspeople are stepping up to satisfy the demand. These days you can buy commercial vegan cookies, brownies, cakes, and more that are practically indistinguishable from their conventional counterparts. While those kinds of vegan treats are fine as fun foods, they often make use of refined sugars, flours, and margarine, which bring their own host of health and environmental concerns. The treats in this book will help you move in a healthier direction as you create sweet vegan treats with whole-grain flours, sweeteners that are less refined, and natural oils—vegan treats that will satisfy a sweet tooth while delivering some nutrition, as well. So not only will you be avoiding butter and eggs, you'll also be eating high-fiber, antioxidant-rich whole grains and healthier sweeteners. How great is that?

Vegan baking has its challenges, especially if you're accustomed to using conventional ingredients. When you bake without eggs, butter, milk, or other dairy products, you must find other ingredients to provide the same baking qualities.

In the case of eggs, every egg is essentially two ingredients: one part from the white, and the other from the yolk. When beaten, the whites provide structure by trapping the gases made by yeast and other leavening agents. They also bind the ingredients together like an edible glue and have a drying effect that keeps baked goods from being overly moist. The yolks add richness and function as emulsifiers, which means that they help prevent liquids and fats from separating. Together, the whites and yolks help keep desserts from being crumbly, too dry, or too wet.

Luckily, plant-based ingredients can stand in for eggs, as long as you aren't trying to make meringue or anything else that requires lots of egg whites for loft. For the kind of cookies, breads, and baked goods that have just an egg or two, ground flaxseeds are a good solution. When ground to a fine powder and mixed with liquid, they can provide the structure and binding usually contributed by eggs. A standard substitution for an egg is mixing 1 tbsp of ground flaxseeds with ¼ cup/60 ml of water. I prefer to use golden flaxseeds for aesthetic reasons and have found that grinding them fresh is best. Grind them in a coffee or spice grinder until they are a fine powder, then whisk them with water or another liquid and let stand for a few minutes, until thickened. The ground seeds will soak in some liquid and form a gel. In many of these recipes, the ground flaxseeds are mixed with the other liquids, so you don't need to whisk them with water. Flaxseeds have the bonus of adding healthful fiber and essential fats.

Powdered egg replacers, which use a mixture of starches and leaveners to mimic the properties of eggs, are another option. There are several brands available, made with different ingredients, used in different quantities, and mixed with water in varying ratios. I tested the recipes in this book using Ener-G brand egg replacer, which is the most widely available, so that's what I call for. It's convenient and works well, especially when you want something that disappears completely into the crumb. Some recipes work best with a combination of flaxseeds and powdered egg replacer standing in for the eggs.

When using these gels and starches for binding, be aware that they need to cool completely to fully set. If a recipe says to cool completely or even chill after baking, try to restrain yourself from cutting into it too soon. The structure of the baked good will be best when it has had time for steam to carry away moisture, resulting in a better texture.

In a few of these recipes, I've used a bit of gluten flour as a binder. This gives baked goods some of the structure that eggs would have provided in a nonvegan version.

However, too much gluten or overworked gluten will make the final product tough, so only use as much as directed, and stir or mix with a light hand.

Once the leavening and binding properties of eggs are taken care of, many vegan recipes for baked goods will also benefit from the moisture and bulk provided by applesauce, pumpkin purée, or puréed tofu. These ingredients can stand in for both eggs and fat, creating a very satisfying richness and heft. Pumpkin and apple-sauce also add sweetness and appealing, familiar flavors that help them stand in for the characteristic tastes of eggs or butter.

You can also learn to bake without butter. Of course, all sorts of healthful fats can be used in baking. For the mouthfeel of butter, coconut oil is a great ingredient. Because it is solid when chilled, it can be grated and added to dry ingredients to simulate cutting in butter or lard, resulting in a flaky crust. Baked goods made with coconut oil have a buttery density, especially when chilled. If you prefer, you can substitute Earth Balance or a similar vegan margarine for coconut oil in most cases. Many vegetable oils are excellent for baking. Canola oil is the default in many of these recipes, but you can use any neutral vegetable oil to achieve the same results. Alternatively, you can try flavorful nut oils for a boost in flavor or olive oil for a distinctive nuance.

Milk is the easiest dairy product to replace. So Delicious brand coconut-based milk has a mild, sweet taste and a relatively thick consistency that makes it a great choice for replacing milk in baked goods. Rice, soy, almond, hazelnut, hemp, and other milks also have their charms, and all should produce similar results if you use them in these recipes. Nondairy milks vary brand to brand; some are thicker and some taste more like their base ingredient. Try a wide variety to discover which you prefer. These recipes were tested using "original" versions of nondairy milks, which are less sweet than vanilla ones. If you use a vanilla version, the final product will just be a little sweeter. There are also unsweetened nondairy milks, which have no added sweeteners and will simply result in a final product that's a little less sweet.

Cream, a fairly common ingredient in traditional sweets, is a bit trickier to replace. When conventional recipes call for cream in sauces or the batter for baked goods, coconut milk or nondairy creamer products work well. Both are richer than nondairy milks. To replace whipped cream, try whipping chilled coconut cream, which can hold some loft if it's ice-cold and whipped quickly. If you want to separate the coconut cream for whipping, be sure to buy a natural brand with no emulsifiers, since you want the coconut milk to separate out into cream and water in the refrigerator. Cashew cream is a simple, elegant solution to the cream question and is easily made from soaked, raw cashews. Simply soak the cashews in water to cover for at least two hours, then drain and blend with just enough fresh water or nondairy milk to yield a velvety smooth purée, which you can sweeten and flavor to taste.

A good replacement for gelatin, which is made from the hooves and tendons of animals, is agar, a gel made from a type of sea vegetable. Agar flakes must be soaked and

simmered to fully dissolve, so be sure to follow the instructions in the recipes in this regard. Agar powder is finer and more easily incorporated but a little more refined, so I only use it in one recipe where the agar must be dissolved quickly. Note that agar can vary in strength from brand to brand and batch to batch, so results may vary.

All the treats in this book will please your healthy heart, your conscience, and your palate as you explore the world of vegan whole-grain fun!

GLOSSARY OF INGREDIENTS

Most of the ingredients used in vegan baking are reassuringly familiar and easy to find wherever you live. That said, there are a few special ingredients that are essential to fabulous vegan baked goods that may be less familiar. If you have questions about any of them, the answers are provided here. Thanks to the Internet and mail order, even items your local shop doesn't carry are just a click or call away.

AGAR   Agar, which is derived from a sea vegetable, is used similarly to gelatin. It is sold in bars, strips, flakes, and powder form and is sometimes referred to as kanten, its Japanese name, which is also the name of the Japanese gelled dessert made using agar. Because it contains 80 percent fiber, some protein, and almost no calories, agar is often recommended when you want to feel full while cutting back on calories.

AGAVE SYRUP   Also known as agave nectar, agave syrup is the sweet sap of one of several kinds of agave plant. It comes in both raw and cooked versions. The raw variety is treated with enzymes; if not labeled "raw," it has been cooked to concentrate the syrup. Agave syrup is naturally high in fructose, which is metabolized more slowly and therefore has a lower glycemic index.

ARROWROOT STARCH   A starch made from a tropical root, arrowroot can be substituted on a one-to-one basis for cornstarch in recipes. It has the benefit of being able to gel more acidic liquids than cornstarch can. Many vegan chefs choose it to avoid both the allergens in corn and genetically modified corn, so often used to make conventional cornstarch.

BROWN RICE SYRUP   To make brown rice syrup, whole brown rice is cooked, then enzymes are added that convert all of the starches in the grain into sugars. Once that is complete, the syrup is strained and cooked to a thick caramel consistency. Brown rice syrup is subtly sweet and can stand in for honey in some recipes.

CANOLA OIL

In recipes that call for a neutral-flavored oil, canola oil is listed in the ingredients, but you can substitute any mildly flavored vegetable oil. I recommend using only organic canola oil, because most of the conventional canola oil in the United States and Canada is made from genetically modified seeds. The label "100%" organic is your only guarantee that an oil is not made from GMO crops. It's also good to seek out expeller-pressed or cold-pressed oils, which have not been heated to high temperatures or extracted with solvents.

CHOCOLATE, VEGAN

Dark chocolate and semisweet chocolate typically don't contain dairy products, but they are made with sugar, which may have been filtered through bone char. If this concerns you, look for chocolates labeled "certified vegan." Another option is grain-sweetened chocolate, which is made with malted grains like barley and corn and no refined sugar. It is mildly sweet and has a slightly stiffer texture when melted.

COCONUT MILK

Coconut milk, which is widely available in cans, can be used as the liquid in recipes, especially those that would be enhanced by a touch of coconut flavor. As always, you'll want to purchase a natural product, but it's especially important with coconut milk if you'd like to separate out the cream to substitute for heavy cream in sauces and baking, and even for whipping. Just refrigerate the can until well chilled, then pour off the thinner, more liquid portion. Be sure to save the coconut water. It can be used as a liquid in many recipes.

COCONUT OIL In the past, coconut oil was greatly maligned because, technically speaking, it consists primarily of saturated fat. However, it differs from other saturated fats because it contains medium-chain triglycerides, which the body metabolizes more like carbohydrates. It also contains lauric acid, which is touted for its antibiotic and anti-fungal properties. It's a great gift to the vegan kitchen because it contributes a mouthfeel that resembles shortening or butter, and because it's more stable and therefore more suitable for high-heat cooking. To measure coconut oil accurately, it should be in liquid form. Melt it by setting it on the back of a hot stove or in a pan of warm water, or by microwaving it (remove the lid first!). To chill it for grating, measure the liquid and then put the measuring cup in the refrigerator for about an hour. Run warm water over the bottom of the cup to loosen the oil.

DRIED CHERRIES, CRANBERRIES, AND OTHER FRUIT When using dried fruit that is very tart in its original state, you may find that it has been sweetened. If you are avoiding white sugar, look for dried fruit that is unsweetened versions or sweetened with fruit juice.

EGG REPLACER POWDER Commercial egg replacer powders are a convenient way to give baked goods some rise and structure. They're typically made with a combination of starches, gums, and leaveners. Just whisk the powder into the amount of liquid specified on the package, being sure to whisk until smooth. All the recipes in this book were tested using Ener-G brand egg replacer, which calls for 1½ tsp powder mixed with 2 tbsp water per egg. If you substitute another brand, you may need to use quantities other than those specified in the recipe. Whichever brand you use, using an egg replacer works best in recipes that don't call for many eggs.

FLAXSEEDS

Flaxseeds are the vegan's friend, providing essential fatty acids that omnivores get from fish, and also standing in for eggs in baking. For each egg you're replacing, whisk together 1 tbsp of finely ground flaxseeds and ¼ cup/60 ml of water.

FRUIT JUICE CONCENTRATES

Canned, frozen fruit juice concentrate can be used as a sweetener in certain preparations. Use neutral juices, like white grape, apple, or pear when making granolas, sauces, or glazes. Note that they tend to be more acidic than other sweeteners, and this can overwhelm some recipes if you use too much.

GLUTEN FLOUR

Gluten is the wheat protein that helps create structure in baked goods. Sometimes called "vital wheat gluten," gluten flour is 75 percent protein and a concentrated source of the protein that gives bread and seitan (often called mock duck, a vegan protein used in stir-fries and savory dishes) their structure. Don't confuse it with high-gluten bread flour, which just has more gluten than regular white flour. Gluten flour is very concentrated so you don't need much in a baked good; for example, just 1 tsp in a whole-wheat bread recipe is sufficient to hold the gases produced by the leavening agents and create some rise, and to stay firm after baking.

JAM AND JELLY, FRUIT-SWEETENED Preserves and spreads labeled as "fruit-sweetened" are just that: fruits cooked with fruit juice concentrates like white grape, pear, and pineapple rather than sugar. These are a great resource for adding wholesome sweetness, as well as the flavor of the base fruit.

MAPLE SYRUP Maple syrup is the concentrated sap of the maple tree, and one of the finest sweeteners you can buy. Grade B maple syrup has a darker hue and more distinctive maple flavor that can enhance recipes. If you prefer pure sweetness, use Grade A.

NONDAIRY MILKS The choices in nondairy milks have exploded in recent years. They are typically made from soy, rice, almonds, oats, and, more recently, hempseeds, coconut, and hazelnuts. Many are now fortified with vitamin B_{12} and other nutrients that may be lacking in a vegan diet. If this is an issue for you, check the label. In most of the recipes in this book, I used sweetened, unflavored nondairy milks (usually labeled as "Original" flavor) to test the recipes, so if you use a sweeter vanilla version, the final product will be a little sweeter. You can also use "unsweetened" versions, in which case the final product won't be quite as sweet.

NUTRITIONAL YEAST This vegan standby is made from deactivated yeast grown on a medium enriched with vitamin B_{12}. Don't confuse it with brewer's yeast, which isn't nearly as tasty. It's available in both flakes and powdered form and has a cheesy flavor that complements many savory dishes. In this book, I use it in a few baked goods to give them a yellow hue and a dairylike taste, as well as a B_{12} boost.

OATS, ROLLED Familiar rolled oats, which usually make their appearance as a breakfast cereal, come in several forms. I'm partial to Bob's Red Mill Extra Thick Rolled Oats for my granolas, but other manufacturers also make hefty old-fashioned rolled oats. Don't use instant or quick oats in the recipes in this book; you won't get the best results. Also, you might be surprised to learn that the smaller and finer the flakes, the higher their glycemic index. A few of the recipes in this book call for oat flour, which you can purchase in most natural food stores. But if you don't have any on hand, simply put some rolled oats in a blender and grind them until powdery.

OLIVE OIL Olive oil is considered one of the healthiest oils. It may surprise you that it has been used in sweets for centuries in the Mediterranean. So many options are available these days. The more buttery, mild varieties are best for baking with; if you aren't sure which variety to purchase, hopefully a knowledgeable salesperson can guide you. You may also enjoy the hint of flavor that comes from baking with stronger flavored extra-virgin oils. Start with the Olive Oil and Date Granola (page 49) and see how you like it.

PALM SUGAR Throughout the tropics, the sap from a variety of palm trees is boiled down to make concentrated sweeteners. When the sap of coconut palms is used, the sugar is sometimes labeled "coconut sugar." Traditionally, it was generally formed into a moist, grainy paste, and this variety is still available, typically in Asian stores, packed in jars or molded into rounds. It has a delicious caramel flavor and is often added to Thai curries and puddings.

As sweeteners go, it's a relatively natural, unprocessed food, somewhat akin to maple syrup, and also has a low glycemic index. Increased interest in palm sugar has led to a dried version becoming available in natural food stores. For the purposes of this book, I'll refer to the moist version as "palm sugar paste" and the dry form as "granular palm sugar." Granular palm sugar is interchangeable with Sucanat or rapadura on a one-to-one basis. Palm sugar paste is easiest to use in recipes where it can be combined with liquids and then heated to melt it. Because it comes in solid form, to measure it by volume you first must chop it, grate it, or mash it. This makes it easier to stir into dry mixtures or helps it dissolve in unheated liquid mixtures. The fresher it is, the softer and easier it is to work with.

PHYLLO DOUGH, WHOLE-WHEAT

Most phyllo dough is made solely with white flour, but in recent years versions that include some whole-wheat flour have become available. Look for whole-wheat phyllo dough in the freezer case at natural food stores. The whole-wheat variety is actually easier to handle because it's a little thicker. Phyllo has a reputation for being tricky to work with, but I've found that thawing it properly makes a huge difference. The day before you want to use it, move it from the freezer to the refrigerator so it thaws slowly. Another challenge with phyllo is that it tends to dry out quickly. You can remedy this by covering the sheets you aren't using with plastic wrap and topping that with a barely damp towel.

SPELT FLOUR

Spelt is an ancient variety of wheat. It does contain gluten, so it isn't suitable for people with celiac disease or with severe wheat allergies. However, people who have only moderate wheat intolerance sometimes find they tolerate spelt fairly well. Whole-spelt flour is lower in gluten than regular whole-wheat bread flour.

SUCANAT Sucanat (a brand name for rapadura sugar) is a great alternative sweetener because it comes in granular dry form like conventional crystalline sugar yet is also relatively unprocessed and higher in nutrients. It's made by pressing whole sugarcane to extract the juice, then boiling and stirring the juice until it forms crumbly bits. No filtration or crystallization is done, and none of the mineral-rich molasses is spun off. It tends to be fairly coarse, so in recipes where a finer texture is required, I call for first blending it until powdery. You can use either a blender or food processor for this.

TOFU Tofu comes in two main forms: regular (usually packaged in water and sold refrigerated) and silken (typically sold in aseptic cartons, but sometimes in refrigerated tubs). Only a few recipes in this book call for tofu, in most cases to stand in for eggs. All call for silken tofu, which is much smoother and wetter than regular tofu.

UNBLEACHED ALL-PURPOSE FLOUR In some of these recipes, I found that using some unbleached wheat flour helped give the final result a better crumb and lighter texture. If you want to go all whole-grain, use white whole-wheat flour and see how you like it.

WHITE WHOLE-WHEAT FLOUR There are many varieties of wheat in the world, but most people only eat one. Break out of the monoculture and try white whole-wheat flour, an excellent flour made from a lighter-colored wheat. It performs much the same and has all the same antioxidants and nutrients as whole-wheat bread flour does, but it's a little lower in gluten. It works well in both yeasted breads and desserts.

WHOLE-WHEAT FLOUR Made from higher-gluten winter wheat, whole-wheat flour is typically used for bread baking. Because of the added bran and germ in the flour, you may want to add a little gluten flour to help your breads achieve loft. It's not as tender in treats like cake or cookies, so use whole-wheat pastry flour when called for in the recipe.

WHOLE-WHEAT PASTRY FLOUR Made from finely ground soft winter wheat, which has a lower gluten content, whole-wheat pastry flour produces tender pastries and baked goods.

A Note on Measuring

Some baking books suggest that you sift flours before measuring. I don't want to do that, and I don't think you do, either. The rationale behind sifting is to get an aerated product that is most uniform in measure; the result is flour that weighs less than flour that's simply scooped out of a container. My method, and that of many bakers, is a compromise. Instead of sifting, scoop the flour with a cup or any other utensil, or even with your hand, then gently shake it into the measuring cup. Tap to make sure there aren't empty spots, then level the top with the back of a knife or any straight edge. This cup of flour will weigh more than a cup of sifted flour, but less than a cup that you scoop right out of the bag, which packs the flour.

SWEET
BREAKFAST
TREATS

We've all heard repeatedly that breakfast is the most important meal of the day, yet so many people still don't eat breakfast. And those who do often eat foods with little or no nutritional value, like donuts and sugary cereals. Breakfast sets the tone for your day, so try to make enjoying a genuinely healthful and delicious breakfast a priority.

I'm not saying you have to give up things that are a little sweet for breakfast if that's what you crave. This is a sweets book, after all. The important thing is to be sure that you nourish yourself with whole foods, and especially whole grains, which are the perfect food to start your day. Their high-fiber, slow-burning complex carbohydrates give you the kind of energy that you need to get moving—and then keep going—without the jarring blood sugar spikes you can get from refined sugars and refined grains. Getting into a routine of eating grains for breakfast also helps gives your digestive system a nice rhythm, with a regular meal of high-antioxidant fiber to start each day.

This isn't about sacrifice. All the breakfast treats you'll find in this chapter are tasty as well as hearty. Give your usual oatmeal or boxed cereal a break and make a rice porridge or completely fuss-free muesli for a change. Or if you're looking for convenience, try the homemade granola recipes. And when you have time and the inclination, and maybe a crowd to feed, branch out with pancakes that pack whole-grain goodness into a fluffy fruit- or nut-studded delight, or a nifty and unconventional breakfast polenta.

If you exercise in the mornings, or if you just don't have time to sit down to a meal, you'll love the recipes for granola bars, breakfast cookies, and energy bars. They make for a small, easily digestible meal before all that cardio—or computer programming, or whatever challenges you face. Their packable nature takes them beyond breakfast, and you'll be saved from stomach-growling hunger on a bike ride or long commute if you have one on hand. They may not last for months like store-bought bars, but they are so much more delicious that there is no comparison.

Pomegranate and Dried Blueberry Muesli

Muesli is a simple way to enjoy whole grains in the morning without having to cook them. Simply stir the oats and liquids together the previous evening. Overnight, the oats will soak up the juice and nondairy milk, making for a soft, supremely enjoyable breakfast cereal.

Serves 4

INGREDIENTS

2 cups/480 ml pomegranate juice

1 cup/240 ml vanilla nondairy milk

2½ cups/250 g thick rolled oats

½ cup/85 g dried blueberries

Nuts, if desired

METHOD

In a storage container with a lid, combine the pomegranate juice, non-dairy milk, oats, blueberries, and nuts (if using). Stir until well mixed. Cover and refrigerate for 4 to 12 hours. Serve cold, or warm the muesli in the microwave or on the stovetop.

Pine Nut Polenta with Cherry Sauce

This polenta, enhanced with your choice of ancient grains and liberally doused with sweet cherries, makes for a fun and tasty breakfast. This method, in which you prepare the polenta the day before, chill it, and then fry or bake it the next morning, results in a slab with crispy edges, essentially giving your hot cereal some texture and visual appeal!

Serves 4 to 6

INGREDIENTS

Polenta

1 cup/140 g coarse cornmeal

3 cups/720 ml water

1 cup/200 g amaranth or teff (or 1 cup/140 g additional coarse cornmeal)

1 cup/240 ml vanilla nondairy milk

½ cup/55 g pine nuts, toasted (see Tip, page 59)

Sauce

10 oz/280 g frozen dark cherries

½ cup/120 ml maple syrup

½ cup/120 ml apple juice

1 tbsp cornstarch

METHOD

Oil a 9-by-5-in/23-by-12-cm loaf pan.

To make the polenta: Put the cornmeal in a medium saucepan, then add the water gradually while whisking continuously. Whisk in the amaranth. Bring to a boil over medium heat, then cook, whisking continuously, until thick, about 5 minutes. Whisk in the nondairy milk and cook, stirring frequently, until very thick, 5 to 10 minutes. Stir in half of the pine nuts.

Scrape the polenta into the prepared pan and spread it in an even layer. Sprinkle the remaining pine nuts on the top and press to adhere. Cover tightly and refrigerate for at least 4 hours, until firm.

To make the sauce: In a small saucepan, combine the cherries and maple syrup. Bring to a boil over medium heat. Lower the heat to maintain a simmer. In a cup or small bowl, whisk the apple juice and cornstarch together until smooth, then stir the mixture into the cherries. Cook until shiny and thickened, about 5 minutes.

Slice the polenta and either fry it in a lightly oiled, well-seasoned cast-iron skillet or bake it on an oiled baking sheet at 400°F/200°C/gas 6 for 10 to 15 minutes, until heated through and browned. Serve topped with the warm sauce, reheating it if need be. Stored in separate airtight containers, the polenta and cherry sauce will keep for about 1 week.

Sweet Congee with Black, Red, and Brown Rices and Asian Pear

Congee is a traditional savory rice porridge often eaten in China. It's usually made with white rice, but this recipe features a trio of whole rices, which will be more filling and give you more sustained energy than white rice. You can make this with just one of the three types of rice listed if that's all that you have on hand. I've given you three options on the cooking method, but be aware that the minimum cooking time is over an hour, so plan ahead.

Serves 5

INGREDIENTS

4½ cups/1 L water

¼ cup/55 g black rice

¼ cup/55 g red rice

½ cup/105 g short-grain brown rice

1 slice fresh ginger

1 tbsp agave syrup or maple syrup

2½ cups/600 ml julienned Asian pears or apples

METHOD

Cooking Option 1
In a slow cooker, combine the water, rices, and ginger. Bring to a boil at high heat, then reduce the heat to low and cook for 5 hours. The rice grains should be exploded and the mixture should have the consistency of thin porridge.

Cooking Option 2
In a medium saucepan, combine the water, rices, and ginger. Bring to a boil at high heat, then reduce the heat to low and cook for 1 hour. The rice grains should be expanded and the mixture should have the consistency of thin porridge.

Cooking Option 3
To speed the prep time in the morning, cook the rices on the stovetop the night before. Combine 2 cups/480ml of the water, the rice, and ginger. Bring to a boil over high heat, then lower the heat, cover, and simmer for 40 minutes, until all the water is absorbed. Cool, cover, and refrigerate overnight. The next morning, add the remaining 2½ cups/600ml water and bring to a boil over high heat. Lower the heat and simmer, stirring frequently, for about 20 minutes. Remove from the heat.

Stir the rice vigorously, then stir in the agave syrup. Serve hot, in 1-cup/240-ml portions, with ½ cup/120 ml of the pears atop each serving.

Olive Oil and Date Granola

Olive oil is so delicious and nutritionally superior, we really ought to use it in more baked goods. This granola will have a hint of olive oil flavor if you use a stronger-tasting one, or if you choose a mild olive oil, its flavor will hardly be noticeable.

Makes 6 cups/1.4 L

INGREDIENTS

4 cups/400 g rolled oats

1 cup/145 g raw almonds, coarsely chopped

Grated zest of 1 large orange

½ cup/120 ml agave syrup

¼ cup/60 ml extra-virgin olive oil

¼ cup/60 ml fresh orange juice

¼ tsp salt

1 cup/170 g pitted dates, coarsely chopped

METHOD

Preheat the oven to 300°F/150°C/gas 2. Oil two rimmed baking sheets.

In a large bowl, combine the oats, almonds, and orange zest. In a medium bowl, combine the agave syrup, olive oil, orange juice, and salt and whisk until thoroughly blended. Pour into the oat mixture and stir until thoroughly combined.

Spread the mixture on the prepared baking sheets. Bake for 50 minutes, rotating the pans and turning the granola with a spatula after 30 minutes of baking. The granola will be quite golden and toasted looking.

Sprinkle half of the dates over each pan of hot granola and mix well. Cool completely on the baking sheets before transferring to an airtight container or zip-top bags. Stored at room temperature, the granola will keep for about 2 weeks.

Coconut-Banana Granola

Coconut milk and dried coconut give this granola wonderful richness and texture. Their tropical flavor is further enhanced by the addition of banana.

Makes 12 cups/2.8 L

INGREDIENTS

6 cups/600 g rolled oats

1 cup/90 g unsweetened shredded dried coconut

½ cup/65 g whole-wheat flour

¼ tsp salt

1 banana

1 cup/240 ml coconut milk

½ cup/120 ml coconut oil

½ cup/100 g granular palm sugar, palm sugar paste (see Tip), or Sucanat

2 tbsp ground flaxseeds

½ tsp coconut extract

½ tsp almond extract

METHOD

Preheat the oven to 300°F/150°C/gas 2. Lightly oil two rimmed baking sheets.

In a large bowl, combine the oats, dried coconut, flour, and salt and stir until well mixed. In a food processor, purée the banana. Add the coconut milk, coconut oil, sugar, flaxseeds, coconut extract, and almond extract and process until thoroughly combined. Pour into the oat mixture and mix well; your hands may work best for this.

Distribute the mixture over the prepared baking sheets, squeezing to form loose clumps. Bake for 1 hour, rotating the pans and turning the granola with a spatula every 20 minutes. The granola will be browned but still feel soft; it will crisp up as it cools.

Cool completely on the baking sheets before transferring to an airtight container or zip-top bags. Stored at room temperature, the granola will keep for about 2 weeks.

TIP To measure palm sugar paste by volume, first chop, mash, or grate it, then pack it into a measuring cup. This makes it easier to stir the palm sugar into dry mixtures or helps it dissolve in unheated liquid mixtures.

Pumpkin-Spice Granola

If you love pumpkin pie, this is the granola for you. Douse it in creamy nut milk and savor the pumpkin-spice flavors as the crisp granola gets soft and chewy. This granola makes a great holiday gift; pack it in a jar or even just in a baggie.

Makes 12 cups/2.8 L

INGREDIENTS

6 cups/600 g rolled oats

½ cup/55 g oat flour, or ½ cup/65 g whole-wheat flour

½ tsp salt

1 cup/240 ml apple juice concentrate, thawed

¾ cup/150 g granular palm sugar, palm sugar paste (see Tip, page 50), or Sucanat

½ cup/120 ml canola oil

½ cup/125 g pumpkin purée (see Tip, page 93)

2 tbsp ground flaxseeds

1 tbsp pumpkin pie spice

1 tsp vanilla extract

1 cup/115 g walnuts, coarsely chopped

METHOD

Preheat the oven to 300°F/150°C/gas 2. Lightly oil two rimmed baking sheets.

In a large bowl, combine the oats, flour, and salt and stir until well mixed. In a food processor, combine the apple juice concentrate, sugar, canola oil, pumpkin purée, flaxseeds, pumpkin pie spice, and vanilla and process until thoroughly combined. Pour into the oat mixture, add the walnuts, and mix well; your hands may work best for this.

Distribute the mixture over the prepared baking sheets, squeezing to form loose clumps. Bake for 70 minutes, rotating the pans and turning the granola with a spatula every 20 minutes. The granola will be quite browned but still feel soft; it will crisp up as it cools.

Cool completely on the baking sheets before transferring to an airtight container or zip-top bags. Stored at room temperature, the granola will keep for about 2 weeks.

Maple-Almond Granola

When you buy maple granola at the store, chances are there is just a whisper of maple syrup and a bunch of sugar, perhaps augmented by some maple flavoring. Here's a recipe so you can make your own and be sure that all of the ingredients are of the highest quality and nothing fake is masquerading as a whole food.

Makes 10 cups/2.4 L

INGREDIENTS

4 cups/400 g rolled oats

1 cup/145 g raw almonds, coarsely chopped

½ cup/55 g raw wheat germ

½ cup/65 g whole-wheat flour

½ tsp salt

1 cup/240 ml maple syrup

¼ cup/60 ml canola oil

2 tsp vanilla extract

½ tsp almond extract

METHOD

Preheat the oven to 300°F/150°C/gas 2. Lightly oil two rimmed baking sheets.

In a large bowl, combine the oats, almonds, wheat germ, flour, and salt and stir until well mixed. In a medium bowl, combine the maple syrup, canola oil, vanilla, and almond extract and whisk until thoroughly blended. Pour into the oat mixture and mix well; your hands may work best for this.

Distribute the mixture over the prepared baking sheets, squeezing to form loose clumps. Bake for 50 minutes, rotating the pans and turning the granola with a spatula after 30 minutes of baking. The granola will be browned but still feel soft; it will crisp up as it cools.

Cool completely on the baking sheets before transferring to an airtight container or zip-top bags. Stored at room temperature, the granola will keep for about 2 weeks.

Peanut Butter and Chocolate Chip Granola Bars

On those days when it's too hot to turn on the oven, you can still make these no-bake granola bars. The simple stovetop method is easy enough for kids to do. Just make sure that the chocolate chips and peanuts are frozen, so they don't soften when you mix everything together.

Makes 9 bars

INGREDIENTS

2 cups/200 g rolled oats

1 cup/30 g crisp brown rice cereal

2 tbsp whole-wheat flour

Pinch of salt

½ cup/120 ml brown rice syrup

2 tbsp palm sugar paste (see Tip, page 50), granular palm sugar, or Sucanat

½ cup/125 g crunchy peanut butter

½ tsp vanilla extract

½ cup/85 g vegan chocolate chips, frozen

½ cup/55 g roasted, unsalted peanuts, frozen

METHOD

Oil a 9-in/23-cm square baking pan.

In a large, dry skillet over medium-high heat, swirl the oats until fragrant and toasted, about 3 minutes. Immediately transfer to a large bowl to prevent burning. Add the brown rice cereal, flour, and salt and stir until well mixed.

In a small saucepan over medium-high heat, combine the brown rice syrup and sugar. Bring to a boil, then lower the heat and simmer for 1 minute. Remove from the heat. Add the peanut butter and vanilla and stir until smooth. Pour into the oat mixture and stir until thoroughly combined. Stir in the chocolate chips and peanuts.

Scrape the mixture into the prepared pan and, using wet hands, press it in an even layer.

Cover with plastic wrap and refrigerate for at least 3 hours. Cut 3 by 3, to make 9 squares. Stored in an airtight container in the refrigerator, the granola bars will keep for about 2 weeks.

Cranberry-Spice Granola Bars

These bars combine the allure of crunchiness with a bit of chewiness, thanks to brown rice syrup and its caramel qualities. Although this recipe calls for warming spices and dried cranberries, you can substitute other dried fruits, from raisins to dried blueberries, to suit your taste.

Makes 24 bars

INGREDIENTS

¼ cup/60 ml nondairy milk

1 tbsp ground flaxseeds

3 cups/300 g rolled oats

1 cup/200 g Sucanat

1 cup/170 g dried cranberries

¼ cup/35 g spelt flour or whole-wheat pastry flour

½ tsp salt

1 tsp ground cinnamon

¼ tsp ground cloves

¼ tsp ground allspice

¼ cup/60 ml canola oil

¼ cup/60 ml brown rice syrup

1 tsp vanilla extract

METHOD

Preheat the oven to 350°F/180°C/gas 4. Line a 13-by-9-in/33-by-23-cm baking pan with parchment paper, allowing some extra length at both ends to help lift the baked bars out of the pan.

In a medium bowl, whisk the nondairy milk and flaxseeds together and let stand for 5 minutes.

In a large bowl, combine the oats, Sucanat, cranberries, spelt flour, salt, cinnamon, cloves, and allspice and stir until well mixed.

Add the canola oil, brown rice syrup, and vanilla to the flaxseed mixture and whisk until thoroughly blended. Pour into the oat mixture and stir until thoroughly combined.

Scrape the mixture into the prepared pan and, using wet hands, press it in an even layer. Bake for 35 to 40 minutes, until golden brown.

Transfer the pan to a wire rack to cool for 5 minutes. Lift the bars out using the parchment paper and, while they are still warm, cut 4 by 6, to make 24 bars. Let cool completely. Stored in an airtight container in the refrigerator, the granola bars will keep for about 2 weeks.

Cocoa-Almond Granola Bars

Of all the granola bars in this book, these are the most cookielike, so if you are craving a cookie, they will ring all those bells. Thick and chewy, they are laced with almonds for a supremely satisfying breakfast or snack.

Makes 16 bars

INGREDIENTS

1½ cups/150 g rolled oats

¾ cup/100 g whole-wheat pastry flour

¼ cup/20 g Dutch-process cocoa powder

¼ tsp baking soda

½ cup/120 ml brown rice syrup

½ cup/100 g granular palm sugar or Sucanat

¼ cup/65 g almond butter

2 tbsp ground flaxseeds

2 tbsp canola oil

1 tbsp nondairy milk

1 tsp vanilla extract

¼ tsp almond extract

¼ cup/30 g slivered almonds

METHOD

Preheat the oven to 350°F/180°C/gas 4. Lightly oil an 8-in/20-cm square baking pan.

In a medium bowl, combine the oats, flour, cocoa powder, and baking soda. In a food processor or large bowl, combine the brown rice syrup, sugar, almond butter, flaxseeds, canola oil, nondairy milk, vanilla, and almond extract and process or stir vigorously until thoroughly blended. Pour into the oat mixture, then knead to make a stiff dough.

Scrape the mixture into the prepared pan and, using wet hands, press it in an even layer. Sprinkle the almonds evenly over the top, then press them in. Bake for 30 to 35 minutes, until puffed up and darker around the edges.

While the bars are still warm, cut 4 by 4, to make 16 squares. Let cool completely. Run a table knife around the edges to loosen the bars, then remove with a spatula. Wrap the bars individually. Stored in an airtight container in the refrigerator, the granola bars will keep for 1 week.

The Power of Flaxseeds

Many of the recipes in this book use flaxseeds to replace eggs, taking full advantage of a glutinous (not gluten!) combination of starch and fiber that the seeds contain in abundance. The magic of flaxseeds extends beyond just a handy glue, though. Each tsp of the tiny seeds contains 570 mg of alpha-linolenic acid, one of the extremely healthful omega-3 fatty acids that we all need to eat every day. However, flaxseeds are also recommended for people who are constipated, so don't overdo it!

Quinoa-Date Energy Bars

Quinoa is a nearly perfect food, offering a delicious combination of easily digestible plant protein, B vitamins, and calcium and other minerals. Adding it to these tasty energy bars gives you a burst of healthful whole-grain energy in every bite. If you like, you can form the mixture into balls and roll them in the 3 tbsp of oats rather than making bars.

Makes 12 bars

INGREDIENTS

3 tbsp plus ¼ cup/25 g rolled oats

1¼ cups/210 g pitted dates (see Tip)

¼ cup/30 g walnuts

¼ cup/30 g ground flaxseeds

3 tbsp Dutch-process cocoa powder

2 tbsp tahini

6 tbsp/90 ml cooked quinoa (see Tip)

METHOD

Oil a 9-by-5-in/23-by-12-cm loaf pan or an 8-in/20-cm square baking pan. Sprinkle the 3 tbsp oats evenly over the surface of the pan.

In a food processor, combine the dates, walnuts, flaxseeds, ¼ cup/25 g oats, cocoa, and tahini and pulse until very finely minced. Press a bit of the mixture in your hand to see if it holds together; if it's crumbly, add 1 tbsp water and process until smooth. Add the quinoa and pulse until thoroughly combined.

Scrape the mixture into the prepared pan and, using wet hands, press it in an even layer. Cover with wax paper and refrigerate until well chilled, about 2 hours.

Cut in 12 bars and wrap them individually. Stored in an airtight container in the refrigerator, the bars will keep for about 2 weeks.

TIP It isn't practical to cook just the small amount of quinoa called for in this recipe. That's no problem; go ahead and cook plenty and use the leftovers as a side dish or as the base for an easy meal some other time. To cook quinoa, combine one and a half parts water and one part quinoa in a saucepan over medium-high heat. Bring to a boil, then lower the heat, cover, and simmer for about 15 minutes, until all of the water is absorbed.

Let it cool for a few minutes before measuring out the amount needed for this recipe. (Cooking 1 cup of quinoa in this way yields about 3 cups of cooked grain.)

If the dates aren't moist and flexible, pour boiling water over them and let soak for 10 minutes to plump them up, then drain.

Espresso and Nut Butter Chunks

If you need a little more pick-me-up than fruit provides, these yummy nuggets are for you. Laced with finely ground whole coffee beans, they deliver a caffeine kick along with the energy from the nuts and fruit.

Makes 24 chunks

INGREDIENTS

2 tbsp oat flour

1 cup/170 g soft dried apricots

½ cup/125 g cashew or almond butter

2 tbsp apple juice concentrate

½ cup/50 g rolled oats

2 tbsp Dutch-process cocoa powder

4 tsp finely ground coffee beans, preferably espresso roast

½ cup/55 g sliced almonds, toasted (see Tip)

METHOD

Oil a 9-by-5-in/23-by-12-cm loaf pan and sprinkle with about 1 tbsp of the flour.

In a food processor, combine the apricots, cashew butter, and apple juice concentrate and process until smooth. Add the oats, cocoa powder, and ground coffee and process until smooth. Press a bit of the mixture in your hand to see if it holds together; if it's crumbly, add 1 tbsp water and process until smooth.

Scrape the mixture into a bowl. Add the almonds and knead them in.

Transfer to the prepared pan and, using wet hands, press in an even layer. Sprinkle the remaining flour evenly over the top. Cover with wax paper and refrigerate until chilled.

Cut 3 by 8, to make 24 squares. Stored in an airtight container in the refrigerator, they will keep for about 2 weeks.

TIP To toast nuts and seeds, preheat the oven to 300°F/150°C/gas 2. Spread the nuts or seeds on a rimmed baking sheet and bake until lightly toasted, from 8 to 15 minutes, depending on the size of the nut. Stir frequently so they'll cook evenly, and keep a close eye on them so they don't burn.

Cherry-Almond Snackers

These easy-to-make treats are quick to eat as you head out the door for a walk or bike ride. Plus, they're packed with energy to fuel you along the way and are very digestible so they won't weigh you down. Be sure to pack one for the trip back!

Makes 4 bars

INGREDIENTS

2 tbsp oat flour

½ cup/85 g pitted moist dates (see Tip, page 58)

2 tbsp almond butter

½ cup/85 g dried cherries

¼ cup/30 g sliced almonds, toasted (see Tip, page 59)

METHOD

Oil a 9-by-5-in/23-by-12-cm loaf pan and sprinkle with about 1 tbsp of the flour.

In a food processor, combine the dates and almond butter and process until smooth. Add the cherries and process again until smooth.

Scrape the mixture into a medium bowl. Add the almonds and knead them in.

Transfer to the prepared pan and, using wet hands, press in an even layer. Sprinkle the remaining flour evenly over the top. Cover with wax paper and refrigerate until well chilled, about 3 hours.

Cut crosswise into 4 bars and wrap them individually. Stored in an airtight container in the refrigerator, the bars will keep for about 2 weeks.

Oatmeal-Raisin Breakfast Cookies

Sneaky bakers know, slip some healthful tofu into a cookie here and there and don't announce it. Sure, it's good to tell people if they need to know, but otherwise let them enjoy the cookie with no preconceptions, then share the secret.

Makes 12 big cookies

INGREDIENTS

1 cup/130 g whole-wheat pastry flour

1 cup/100 g rolled oats

1 tsp salt

1 tsp baking soda

2 tsp ground cinnamon

6 oz/170 g silken tofu, drained

½ cup/120 ml maple syrup

2 tbsp ground flaxseeds

1½ tsp vanilla extract

1 cup/170 g raisins

1 cup/135 g pecans, coarsely chopped

METHOD

Preheat the oven to 350°F/180°C/gas 4.

In a large bowl, combine the flour, oats, salt, baking soda, and cinnamon and stir until well mixed.

In a blender or food processor, purée the tofu. Scrape down the sides and process again until completely smooth. Add the maple syrup, flaxseeds, and vanilla and process until very smooth. Scrape the mixture into the flour mixture and stir until well combined. Stir in the raisins and pecans.

To form each cookie, scoop a scant ¼-cup/60-ml portion of dough (oiling the measuring cup makes it easier to remove the dough) and form it into a ball. Place the balls on an ungreased baking sheet, leaving about 3 in/7.5 cm of space between them. Using wet palms, flatten the balls to a thickness of about ½ in/12 mm.

Bake for 16 minutes, until golden brown and firm, rotating the pan halfway through the baking time.

Let cool on the pan for 5 minutes, then transfer to a wire rack to cool completely. Stored in an airtight container in the refrigerator, the cookies will keep for 1 week.

Hazelnut-Carrot Breakfast Cookies

Toasted hazelnuts, also known as filberts, have such a delicious flavor. Skinning them takes a few minutes, but tastes better in the final result. If you don't mind the skins, you can skip that step. Another alternative is to substitute another nut, like walnuts, that taste just as delicious but don't have to be skinned.

Makes about 28 small cookies

INGREDIENTS

1 cup/130 g whole-wheat pastry flour

1 tbsp ground flaxseeds

1 tsp baking powder

½ tsp salt

½ cup/120 ml agave syrup

¼ cup/65 g almond butter

¼ cup/60 ml canola oil

1 cup/110 g shredded carrots

½ cup/60 g hazelnuts, toasted and skinned
(see Tip) and coarsely chopped

METHOD

Preheat the oven to 350°F/180°C/gas 4. Line a baking sheet with parchment paper or oil it lightly.

In a large bowl, combine the flour, flaxseeds, baking powder, and salt and whisk until well mixed. In a medium bowl, combine the agave syrup, almond butter, and canola oil and stir vigorously until smooth and well mixed. Pour into the flour mixture and stir until well combined. Stir in the carrots and hazelnuts.

Scoop the dough onto the prepared baking sheet, using a heaping 1 tbsp per cookie and leaving about 3 in/7.5 cm of space between them.

Bake for about 15 minutes, until golden around the edges and puffed up, rotating the pan halfway through the baking time.

Let cool on the pan for 5 minutes, then transfer to a wire rack to cool completely. Stored in an airtight container in the refrigerator, the cookies will keep for 1 week.

TIP To toast and skin hazelnuts, spread them on a baking sheet and bake at 350°F/180°C/gas 4 for 15 minutes, stirring them after 10 minutes of baking. Put the nuts on a dish towel, wrap it around them, and rub to remove the skins. Some bits of skin may remain stuck to the hazelnuts, which is fine. If a fair amount of skins won't come off, you can try baking the stubborn hazelnuts for a few minutes longer, keeping a watchful eye on them to prevent burning.

Coconut-Mango Breakfast Cookies

Crunchy, chewy nuggets of breakfast like these are always popular, especially when enhanced with tropical flavors, so be sure to have extras on hand to share. They are kind of like a portable bowl of oats and fruit, with a boost of protein from the almond butter.

Makes about 11 big cookies

INGREDIENTS

1½ cups/150 g rolled oats

1 cup/90 g unsweetened shredded dried coconut

¼ cup/35 g whole-wheat pastry flour

½ tsp baking soda

¼ tsp salt

¼ cup/65 g almond butter

2 ripe bananas, mashed

¼ cup/60 ml agave syrup

1 tsp vanilla extract

½ tsp coconut extract

1 cup/240 g chopped dried mango

METHOD

Preheat the oven to 350°F/180°C/gas 4.

In a large bowl, combine the oats, coconut, flour, baking soda, and salt and whisk until well mixed. In a food processor or medium bowl, combine the almond butter and bananas and process or stir vigorously until thoroughly blended. Stir in the agave syrup, vanilla, and coconut extract. Pour into the oat mixture and stir until well combined, then stir in the mango.

To form each cookie, scoop a scant ¼-cup/60-ml portion of the dough (oiling the measuring cup makes it easier to remove the dough) and form it into a ball. Place the balls on an ungreased baking sheet, leaving about 2 in/5 cm of space between them. Using wet palms, flatten the balls to a thickness of about ¾ in/2 cm.

Bake for 20 to 25 minutes, until brown around the edges, rotating the pan halfway through the cooking time.

Let cool on the pan for 5 minutes, then transfer to a wire rack to cool completely. Stored in an airtight container in the refrigerator, the cookies will keep for 1 week.

Maple-Peanut Breakfast Cookies

Peanuts are such a great addition to breakfast, providing protein and healthful fats, while also adding an enticing crunch. In this recipe, maple syrup and peanuts combine in a cookie that will make you forget about packaged granola bars. These simple little cookies pack easily for wherever you might be headed.

Makes about 24 cookies

INGREDIENTS

2 tbsp ground flaxseeds

¼ cup/60 ml nondairy milk

2 cups/260 g whole-wheat pastry flour

½ tsp baking soda

¼ tsp salt

1 cup/240 ml maple syrup

¼ cup/60 ml peanut or canola oil

¼ cup/65 g crunchy peanut butter

½ tsp vanilla extract

1 cup/115 g roasted, unsalted peanuts, coarsely chopped

METHOD

Preheat the oven to 350°F/180°/gas 4. Line two baking sheets with parchment paper or oil them lightly.

In a cup or small bowl, whisk the flaxseeds and nondairy milk and let stand for 5 minutes.

In a large bowl, combine the flour, baking soda, and salt and whisk until well mixed. In a medium bowl, combine the maple syrup, peanut oil, peanut butter, and vanilla and stir vigorously until thoroughly blended. Stir in the flaxseed mixture, then pour into the flour mixture. Stir until thoroughly combined.

Scoop the dough onto the prepared pan, using about 2 tbsp of dough per cookie and leaving about 2 in/5cm of space between them.

Bake for 16 minutes, until firm to the touch and browned around the edges, rotating the pans halfway through the baking time.

Let cool on the pan for 5 minutes, then transfer to wire racks to cool completely. Stored in an airtight container in the refrigerator, the cookies will keep for 1 week.

Basic Pancakes with Add-Ins

A lovely warm pancake breakfast can be yours in minutes. Just combine the dry ingredients the night before. In the morning, you'll only need to measure the wet ingredients and mix them in. For a special treat, try serving these pancakes topped with a dollop of Cashew Cream (page 107).

Serves 3 or 4

INGREDIENTS

2 cups/480 ml nondairy milk, plus more as needed

¼ cup/30 g ground flaxseeds

2 tsp egg replacer, such as Ener-G

2 cups/260 g whole-wheat flour

¼ cup/50 g Sucanat or granular palm sugar

2 tsp gluten flour

2 tsp baking powder

½ tsp salt

¼ tsp baking soda

2 tbsp canola oil

1 cup/240 ml add-ins, such as berries, chopped nuts, sliced bananas, dried fruit, or granola

Agave syrup or maple syrup for drizzling

METHOD

In a medium bowl, combine the nondairy milk, flaxseeds, and egg replacer and whisk until smooth and frothy. Let stand for 5 minutes.

In a large bowl, combine the flour, Sucanat, flour, baking powder, salt, and baking soda and whisk until well mixed. Whisk the canola oil into the flaxseed mixture, then pour into the flour mixture. Quickly stir until just combined. (If the batter seems thick, cook a single tester pancake first. If it doesn't spread to under ½ in/12 mm thick, stir in a bit more nondairy milk before cooking more pancakes.)

Lightly oil a nonstick frying pan or griddle and set it over medium heat. When the pan is hot, use a ¼-cup/60-ml measure to portion the batter onto the pan, leaving 2 in/5 cm of space between the pancakes. As soon as you portion the batter onto the pan, sprinkle about 1 tbsp of the add-ins on each pancake and push them down with a spatula. Cook until bubbles appear all over the top surface and the edges are dry, 2 to 3 minutes. Flip and cook the other side for about 1 minute. Continue cooking the remaining pancakes in the same way. Serve warm, drizzled with syrup and with any extra add-ins sprinkled over the top.

TIP To serve the pancakes all at once, transfer cooked pancakes to a plate and hold them in an oven preheated to 200°F/95°C/gas ¼ while you cook the remaining pancakes.

Jumbo Buckwheat Pancakes with Strawberry Sauce

The jumbo cakes that you get at the local breakfast place are easy enough to make at home; you just need a large pan and the patience to wait for them to cook through. These buckwheat cakes aren't very sweet; in fact, if you're in the mood for a savory breakfast, forgo the sauce and serve them like a fresh flatbread with a vegan scramble or tempeh bacon.

Serves 6 to 10

INGREDIENTS

Sauce

1 lb/455 g strawberries, sliced

½ cup/120 ml agave syrup

1 tbsp fresh lemon juice

Pancakes

1½ cups/195 g whole-wheat flour

1½ cups/195 g buckwheat flour

2 tsp gluten flour (optional)

1 tsp baking powder

1 tsp baking soda

½ tsp salt

2½ cups/600 ml almond milk or other nondairy milk

1 tbsp egg replacer, such as Ener-G

¼ cup/60 ml agave syrup

1 tbsp fresh lemon juice

METHOD

To make the sauce: In a medium saucepan, combine the strawberries, agave syrup, and lemon juice. Bring to a simmer over medium heat. Lower the heat and continue to simmer, stirring frequently, until the strawberries break down and sauce thickens a bit. Keep warm until ready to serve.

To make the pancakes: In a large bowl combine the three flours, baking powder, baking soda, and salt and whisk until well mixed. In a medium bowl, combine ¼ cup of the almond milk and the egg replacer and whisk until smooth and frothy. Add the remaining 2¼ cups almond milk, the agave syrup, and lemon juice and whisk until thoroughly blended. Pour into the flour mixture and stir just until combined.

Lightly oil two large nonstick frying pans and set them over medium heat. (You can also use one large, rectangular griddle.) When the pan is hot, use a ½-cup/120-ml measure to portion one pancake into each pan; they should spread to a width of 6 to 7 in/15 to 17 cm. Cook until bubbles appear all over the top surface and the edges are dry, 2 to 3 minutes. Flip and cook the other side for about 1 minute. Continue cooking the remaining pancakes in the same way. Serve warm, topped with the strawberry sauce.

TIP To serve the pancakes all at once, transfer cooked pancakes to a plate and hold them in an oven preheated to 200°F/95°C/gas ¼ while you cook the remaining pancakes.

Blueberry and Blue Corn Cakes

Blue cornmeal is a fun change of pace from the standard yellow variety. Though the difference is subtle, it has its own unique flavor, not to mention that pretty purplish hue. It also gives the toasty tops and bottoms of these pancakes a delicate crunch. Go ahead and buy a bag of blue cornmeal for these cakes. I guarantee you'll enjoy trying it in other recipes that call for cornmeal, such as cornbread and muffins.

Serves 4

INGREDIENTS

¾ cup/100 g white whole-wheat flour

¾ cup/120 g blue cornmeal

2 tbsp Sucanat or granular palm sugar

2 tbsp baking powder

1 tsp gluten flour

¼ tsp salt

1 cup/240 ml nondairy milk, plus more as needed

2 tbsp canola oil

1 cup/155 g fresh blueberries

Agave syrup or maple syrup for drizzling

METHOD

In a large bowl, combine the whole-wheat flour, cornmeal, Sucanat, baking powder, gluten flour, and salt and whisk until well mixed. In a medium bowl, whisk the nondairy milk and canola oil together, then pour into the flour mixture. Quickly stir just until combined. (If the batter seems thick, cook a single tester pancake first. If it doesn't spread to under ½ in/12 mm thick, stir in a bit more nondairy milk before cooking more pancakes.)

Lightly oil a nonstick frying pan or griddle and set it over medium heat. When the pan is hot, use a ¼-cup/60-ml measure to portion the batter onto the pan, leaving 2 in/5 cm of space between the pancakes. As soon as you portion the batter into the pan, sprinkle a heaping 1 tbsp of blueberries on each pancake and push them down with a spatula. Cook until bubbles appear all over the top surface and the edges are dry, 2 to 3 minutes. Flip and cook the other side for about 1 minute. Continue cooking the remaining pancakes in the same way. Serve warm, drizzled with syrup.

TIP To serve the pancakes all at once, transfer cooked pancakes to a plate and hold them in an oven preheated to 200°F/95°C/gas ¼ while you cook the remaining pancakes.

Yeasted Cinnamon-Swirl Coffee Cake with Hazelnut Streusel

This cake is like a big spiral of cinnamon rolls, with streusel scattered everywhere. Make sure to let the dough rise until it is nice and fluffy; sometimes doughs made with whole-wheat flour take a little longer to rise than those made with white flour.

Serves 12

INGREDIENTS

6 cups/780 g white whole-wheat flour, or as needed

½ cup/60 g chickpea flour

1 tbsp bread-machine yeast

½ tsp salt

1½ cups/360 ml nondairy milk

½ cup/120 ml canola oil

¼ cup/60 ml brown rice syrup

¼ cup/60 ml agave syrup

METHOD

In a stand mixer or a large bowl, combine 4 cups/520 g of the whole-wheat flour, the chickpea flour, yeast, and salt.

In a small saucepan or the microwave, heat the nondairy milk until steaming. Stir in the canola oil, brown rice syrup, and agave syrup. Measure the temperature; it should be no hotter than 115°F/45°C, or it will kill the yeast.

Pour the liquid mixture into the flour mixture and stir until the dough comes together and all of the flour is incorporated. Using the stand mixer or kneading in the bowl, knead in the remaining flour, ½ cup/65 g at a time, until the dough is soft and still somewhat sticky. Continue kneading for 5 minutes, continuing to add a bit of flour as needed to keep it from sticking.

Oil a large bowl. Transfer the dough to the bowl and cover with plastic wrap or a pan lid. Let rise in a warm place until doubled in size, about 1 hour.

Continued

Streusel

1 cup/200 g Sucanat

½ cup/65 g whole-wheat pastry flour

1 tbsp ground cinnamon

Pinch of salt

1 cup/120 g hazelnuts, toasted and skinned (see Tip, page 63)

½ cup/120 ml coconut oil, melted

To make the streusel: In a blender or food processor, grind the Sucanat until powdery. Add the pastry flour, cinnamon, and salt and process until well mixed. Add the hazelnuts and pulse until coarsely chopped. Transfer to a medium bowl and stir in the canola oil. Press it into a clumpy mixture, cover, and refrigerate.

Preheat the oven to 350°F/180°C/gas 4. Lightly oil a 10-in/25-cm spring-form pan.

When the dough has doubled in size, transfer it to a floured counter and pat it into a 24-by-8-in/60-by-20-cm rectangle. If it starts to resist, let it rest for a few minutes, then continue patting it out.

Set aside one-third of the streusel. Crumble the remaining two-thirds over the dough evenly, leaving a 1-in/2.5-cm border bare. Starting at a long edge, roll up the dough to form a long cylinder. Pinch the seam to seal.

Place the roll in the prepared pan, seam-side down, forming a coil in the pan. Press gently but firmly with your palms to flatten the coil so it fills the pan. Cover and let rise until doubled in size, about 1 hour.

Crumble the remaining streusel over the top, especially in the seams. Bake for about 40 minutes, until the top is golden brown and the cake sounds hollow when tapped.

Transfer to a wire rack to cool and remove the sides of the springform pan. Serve slightly warm or at room temperature. Stored in the refrigerator, tightly covered, the coffee cake will keep for about 1 week.

SCONES, MUFFINS
& QUICK BREADS

If you are looking for an appealing way to eat whole grains, you can hardly imagine one more seductive than a scone, muffin, or quick bread. They entice with their tender, fruit- and nut-studded familiarity and are delicious whether slathered with jams or just snarfed down warm, right off the cooling rack. All these baked goods are quick and easy to make and don't require any special cooking skills.

Scones are of British origin, but Americans have embraced them and done their thing to them, adding in every fruit, nut, and flavoring imaginable. Though it may have started as an unassuming little biscuit to dip in tea, it is now a full-on event of its own. The great thing about scones is that they are already a pretty dense, low-to-the-ground sort of baked good. Making vegan, whole-grain versions doesn't significantly change the character of what has always been a hefty little wedge. That's what we love about them, and these scones don't disappoint. But instead of loads of butter and cream, they derive their moistness from ingredients like applesauce and pumpkin purée, and coconut oil and other oils keep them just rich enough to ring those scone bells.

Who doesn't love muffins? Yet nutritionists often warn us about them, and rightfully so. Even when store-bought versions seem to be full of whole grains and other healthful ingredients, that's often just a fake-out. A quick read of the ingredients list will expose their white flour and sugar content. Rest assured that the muffins in this chapter are packed with real, whole foods and intense, satisfying flavors. They're nutritious and hearty, and you may find that just one will suffice for a complete breakfast or lunch.

Quick bread loaves have a nostalgic appeal, especially if your mother or grandmother baked banana bread during the holidays or zucchini bread at the end of summer to help use up a bountiful harvest. There was never any left over to go stale at our house, I promise you. They are also a vegan parent's best friend; a single, easily prepared loaf can serve as a week's worth of after-school snacks or peanut butter–smeared breakfasts—with no butter or eggs in sight.

Apple-Pecan Scones

These scones have great apple flavor, thanks to the combination of applesauce, which is used in place of eggs, and chopped apples. Apples are available year-round, and pecans provide the perfect contrast in texture and flavor.

Makes 8 scones

INGREDIENTS

2 cups/260 g whole-wheat pastry flour

1 cup/115 g unbleached all-purpose flour

½ cup/100 g Sucanat, plus 2 tbsp

1 tsp baking powder

1 tsp baking soda

½ tsp salt

1 tsp ground cinnamon

½ cup/120 ml coconut oil, melted

½ cup/120 ml unsweetened applesauce

¼ cup/60 ml nondairy milk

1 tsp apple cider vinegar

1 cup/110 g chopped apple

½ cup/70 g chopped pecans

METHOD

Preheat the oven to 400°F/200°C/gas 6.

In a large bowl, combine both flours, the ½ cup/100 g Sucanat, and the baking powder, baking soda, salt, and cinnamon and whisk until well mixed. In a medium bowl, combine the coconut oil, applesauce, non-dairy milk, and vinegar and whisk until thoroughly blended. Pour into the flour mixture and stir until just combined. Add the apple and pecans and stir until just combined.

Scrape the dough out onto a lightly floured work surface. Form it into a disk, then pat it to a thickness of about 1 in/2.5 cm. Cut into eight wedges. Sprinkle with the 2 tbsp Sucanat and transfer the wedges to an ungreased baking sheet, leaving about 2 in/5 cm of space between them.

Bake for 20 to 25 minutes, until golden and firm. Transfer to a wire rack to cool. Stored in an airtight container at room temperature, the scones will keep for 1 week.

Blueberry-Lemon Scones

Blueberries and lemon are the perfect way to celebrate spring. When the lemony scent of these scones wafts through your house, everyone will want one. Be sure to mix the berries in gently so they don't break and bleed into the dough.

Makes 12 scones

INGREDIENTS

½ cup/100 g Sucanat

1 cup/130 g whole-wheat pastry flour

1 cup/130 g white whole-wheat flour

1 tbsp grated lemon zest

2 tsp baking powder

1 tsp baking soda

½ tsp salt

½ cup/120 ml coconut oil, chilled (see Tip, page 129)

1 tbsp fresh lemon juice

¾ cup/180 ml nondairy milk

1½ cups/230 g fresh blueberries

METHOD

Preheat the oven to 400°F/200°C/gas 6.

In a blender, grind the Sucanat until powdery. Transfer to a large bowl. Add both flours, the lemon zest, baking powder, baking soda, and salt and whisk until well mixed. Grate the chilled coconut oil into the flour mixture, then toss until the bits of coconut oil are evenly coated. Mix gently with your fingers, squeezing to break up the bits and working quickly so the warmth from your hands doesn't melt the coconut oil.

Whisk the lemon juice into the nondairy milk. Pour into the flour mixture and stir until just combined. Add the blueberries and stir gently until just combined.

Scrape the dough onto a lightly floured work surface and divide it into two equal portions. Form each into a disk, then pat them to a thickness of about 1 in/2.5 cm. Cut each into six wedges. Transfer the wedges to an ungreased baking sheet, leaving about 2 in/5 cm of space between them.

Bake for 15 minutes, until golden brown around the edges and firm to the touch. Transfer to wire racks to cool. Stored in an airtight container at room temperature, the scones will keep for about 1 week.

Mocha Scones with Cacao Nibs and Chocolate Chips

These petite scones are a perfect pick-me-up, with a hint of coffee flavor and a double dose of chocolate to pull you out of a slump. Cacao nibs are dry-roasted, cracked cacao beans; they have a flavor and texture reminiscent of roasted coffee beans. If you don't have cacao nibs on hand, you can substitute chopped nuts or more chocolate chips.

Makes 12 scones

INGREDIENTS

3 cups/390 g whole-wheat pastry flour

½ cup/65 g buckwheat flour

1 tsp baking powder

1 tsp baking soda

½ tsp salt

½ cup/120 ml coconut oil, chilled (see Tip, page 129)

¾ cup/180 ml coconut milk

½ cup/120 ml agave syrup

1 tsp apple cider vinegar

1 tsp vanilla extract

1 tsp coffee extract

1 cup/170 g vegan chocolate chips

½ cup/55 g cacao nibs

METHOD

Preheat the oven to 400°F/200°C/gas 6. Lightly oil a baking sheet.

In a large bowl, combine both flours, the baking powder, baking soda, and salt and whisk until well mixed. Grate the chilled coconut oil into the flour mixture, then toss until the bits of coconut oil are evenly coated. Mix gently with your fingers, squeezing to break up the bits and working quickly so the warmth from your hands doesn't melt the coconut oil.

In a medium bowl, combine the coconut milk, agave syrup, vinegar, vanilla, and coffee extract and whisk until thoroughly blended. Pour into the flour mixture and stir until just combined. Add the chocolate chips and cacao nibs and stir until just combined.

Scrape the dough out onto a lightly floured work surface. Form it into a disk, then pat it to a thickness of about 1 in/2.5 cm. Cut into twelve wedges. Transfer the wedges to the prepared baking sheet, leaving about 1 in/2.5 cm of space between them.

Bake for 15 minutes, until the tops are golden brown. Transfer to a wire rack to cool. Stored in an airtight container at room temperature, the scones will keep for about 1 week.

Pumpkin-Cornmeal Scones

Creamy pumpkin, crunchy cornmeal, and tangy cranberries combine to make these scones a perfect fall treat. Pack a few of these to take to work, and enjoy them on your coffee break.

Makes about 8 scones

INGREDIENTS

¾ cup/120 g cornmeal

½ cup/65 g whole-wheat pastry flour

½ cup/60 g unbleached all-purpose flour

1 tbsp baking powder

½ tsp salt

1 tbsp ground cinnamon

¼ cup/60 ml coconut oil, chilled (see Tip, page 129)

1 cup/245 g pumpkin purée

¼ cup/60 ml maple syrup

¼ cup/60 ml nondairy milk

½ cup/85 g dried cranberries

METHOD

Preheat the oven to 400°F/200°C/gas 6. Line a baking sheet with parchment paper or oil it lightly.

In a large bowl, combine the cornmeal, both flours, the baking powder, salt, and cinnamon. Grate the chilled coconut oil into the cornmeal mixture, then toss until the bits of coconut oil are evenly coated. Mix gently with your fingers, squeezing to break up the bits and working quickly so the warmth from your hands doesn't melt the coconut oil.

In a medium bowl, combine the pumpkin purée, maple syrup, and nondairy milk and whisk until well blended. Pour into the cornmeal mixture and stir until just combined. Add the cranberries and stir until just combined.

Scrape the dough out onto a lightly floured work surface. Form it into a disk, then pat it to a thickness of about 1 in/2.5 cm. Cut into eight wedges. Transfer the wedges to the prepared baking sheet, leaving about 2 in/5 cm of space between them.

Bake for 15 to 18 minutes, until golden around the edges and firm to the touch. Transfer to a wire rack to cool. Stored in an airtight container in the refrigerator, the scones will keep for 1 week.

Blood Orange Muffins with Apricots

The zest and juice of blood oranges add scarlet drama to these muffins. Of course, you can substitute other oranges. The muffins will still taste great, even if they don't have the same exotic red tint.

Makes 6 muffins

INGREDIENTS

¼ cup/60 ml nondairy milk

1 tbsp ground flaxseeds

2 cups/260 g whole-wheat pastry flour

1 tbsp grated blood orange zest

1 tsp baking powder

½ tsp baking soda

¼ tsp salt

¾ cup/180 ml maple syrup

¼ cup/60 ml canola oil

¼ cup/60 ml fresh blood orange juice

1 cup/170 g dried apricots, chopped

METHOD

Preheat the oven to 350°F/180°C/gas 4. Line six muffin cups with paper liners, then lightly oil the top of the pan so the muffin tops don't stick.

In a medium bowl, whisk the nondairy milk and flaxseeds together and let stand for 5 minutes.

In a large bowl, combine the flour, orange zest, baking powder, baking soda, and salt and whisk until well mixed.

Add the maple syrup, canola oil, and orange juice to the flaxseed mixture and whisk until thoroughly blended. Pour into the flour mixture and stir until just combined. Add the apricots and stir until just combined; don't overmix or the muffins will be tough.

Scoop the batter into the muffin cups, dividing it evenly among them; they should be about full. Bake for 35 minutes, until the tops are golden brown.

Cool the muffins in the pan for about 10 minutes, then transfer to a wire rack to cool completely. Stored in an airtight container in the refrigerator, the muffins will keep for about 1 week.

Raspberry Muffins

When fresh raspberries are in season, show them off in these tender muffins. The rest of the year, use frozen raspberries and just follow the directions to bake them a little longer. Whether you use fresh or frozen berries, the explosions of tangy, juicy raspberry flavor will be divine!

Makes 12 muffins

INGREDIENTS

3 cups/390 g whole spelt or whole-wheat pastry flour

1½ cups/175 g unbleached all-purpose flour

2 tsp grated lemon zest

2 tsp baking powder

1 tsp baking soda

½ tsp salt

1 cup/240 ml nondairy milk

2 tbsp ground flaxseeds

4 tsp egg replacer, such as Ener-G

½ cup/120 ml brown rice syrup

½ cup/120 ml maple syrup

¼ cup/60 ml canola oil

2 cups/255 g fresh or frozen raspberries

1 tsp arrowroot starch (if using frozen raspberries)

METHOD

Preheat the oven to 350°F/180°C/gas 4. Line twelve muffin cups with paper liners, then lightly oil the top of the pan so the muffin tops don't stick.

In a large bowl, combine both flours, the lemon zest, baking powder, baking soda, and salt and whisk until well mixed. In a medium bowl, whisk the nondairy milk, flaxseeds, and egg replacer together until smooth and frothy. Add the brown rice syrup, maple syrup, and canola oil and whisk until thoroughly combined.

If using frozen berries, get them out of the freezer just before using and, in a medium bowl, toss them with the arrowroot starch.

Pour the liquid mixture into the flour mixture and stir until just combined. Add the berries and gently stir until just combined. Don't overmix or the berries will break down and the muffins will be tough.

Scoop the batter into the muffin cups, dividing it evenly among them; they should be about full. Bake for about 25 minutes if using fresh berries, and about 35 minutes if using frozen berries, until a toothpick inserted in the center of a muffin comes out clean and dry.

Cool the muffins in the pan for about 10 minutes, then transfer to a wire rack to cool completely. Stored in an airtight container in the refrigerator, the muffins will keep for about 1 week.

Righteous Raisin Muffins

This is a great basic muffin recipe that you can easily vary by substituting your favorite dried fruit for the raisins. Using maple sugar chunks on top of the muffins makes for a garnish that's as tasty as it is attractive, but if you don't have any on hand, you can use any type of coarse sugar, or just bake them with their tops gloriously naked.

Makes 6 muffins

INGREDIENTS

6 tbsp/90 ml nondairy milk

1 tbsp ground flaxseeds

¾ cup/100 g whole-wheat pastry flour

½ cup/60 g unbleached all-purpose flour

½ cup/55 g wheat germ

1 tsp baking powder

½ tsp baking soda

¼ tsp salt

¼ cup/60 ml canola oil

¾ cup/180 ml maple syrup or agave syrup

1 cup/170 g raisins

Maple sugar chunks for garnish

METHOD

Preheat the oven to 350°F/180°C/gas 4. Line six muffin cups with paper liners, then lightly oil the top of the pan so the muffin tops don't stick.

In a medium bowl, whisk the nondairy milk and flaxseeds together and let stand for 5 minutes.

In a large bowl, combine both flours, the wheat germ, baking powder, baking soda, and salt and whisk until well mixed.

Add the canola oil and maple syrup to the flaxseed mixture and whisk until thoroughly blended. Pour into the flour mixture and stir until just combined. Add the raisins and stir until just combined; don't overmix or the muffins will be tough.

Scoop the batter into the muffin cups, dividing it evenly among them; they should be about full. Sprinkle a few maple sugar chunks on top of each muffin. Bake for 35 minutes, until the tops are golden brown.

Cool the muffins in the pan for about 10 minutes, then transfer to a wire rack to cool completely. Stored in an airtight container in the refrigerator, the muffins will keep for about 1 week.

Wheat Germ and Carrot Muffins

Wheat germ, with its toothsome texture and hint of sweetness, pairs well with naturally sweet carrots. These hefty muffins, packed with crunchy pecans and other healthful goodies, are a meal in themselves.

Makes 8 muffins

INGREDIENTS

1 cup/240 ml nondairy milk

2 tbsp ground flaxseeds

1 cup/130 g whole-wheat pastry flour

1 cup/110 g raw wheat germ

1½ tsp baking soda

1 tsp baking powder

½ tsp salt

1 ripe banana, mashed

½ cup/100 g palm sugar paste (see Tip, page 50), granular palm sugar, or Sucanat

3 tbsp canola oil

1 cup/110 g shredded carrots

¼ cup/35 g chopped pecans

METHOD

Preheat the oven to 375°F/190°C/gas 5. Line eight muffin cups with paper liners, then lightly oil the top of the pan so the muffin tops don't stick.

In a medium bowl, whisk the nondairy milk and flaxseeds together and let stand for 5 minutes.

In a large bowl, combine the flour, wheat germ, baking soda, baking powder, and salt and whisk until well mixed.

Add the banana, sugar, and canola oil to the flaxseed mixture and stir until thoroughly combined. Pour into the flour mixture and stir until just combined. Add the carrots and pecans and stir until just combined; don't overmix or the muffins will be tough.

Scoop the batter into the muffin cups, dividing it evenly among them; they should be about full. Bake for 30 to 35 minutes, until a toothpick inserted in the center of a muffin comes out clean and dry.

Cool the muffins in the pan for about 10 minutes, then transfer to a wire rack to cool completely. (These muffins are very moist, so it's important that they cool completely before serving.) Stored in an airtight container in the refrigerator, the muffins will keep for 1 week.

Pumpkin and Chocolate Chip Muffins

Pumpkin and chocolate are a perfect combo, making these muffins a moist and delectable treat. These are a bit smaller than some of the other muffins in this book, making them perfect for little hands and mouths.

Makes 12 muffins

INGREDIENTS

¾ cup/100 g whole-wheat pastry flour

¼ cup/30 g unbleached all-purpose flour

½ tsp baking soda

¼ tsp salt

1 tsp ground cinnamon

½ cup/125 g pumpkin purée

¼ cup/60 ml brown rice syrup

½ cup/120 ml rice milk or other nondairy milk

¼ cup/60 ml canola oil

1 tbsp ground flaxseeds

1 cup/100 g vegan chocolate chips

METHOD

Preheat the oven to 375°F/190°C/gas 5. Line twelve muffin cups with paper liners, then lightly oil the top of the pan so the muffin tops don't stick.

In a large bowl, combine both flours, the baking soda, salt, and cinnamon and whisk until well mixed. In a medium bowl, combine the pumpkin purée and brown rice syrup and whisk vigorously until thoroughly combined. Add the rice milk, canola oil, and flaxseeds and whisk until thoroughly blended. Pour into the flour mixture and stir until just combined. Add the chocolate chips and stir until just combined; don't overmix, or the muffins will be tough.

Scoop the batter into the muffin cups, dividing it evenly among them and using a heaping ¼ cup/60 ml of batter per muffin. Bake for 30 to 35 minutes, until a toothpick inserted in the center of a muffin comes out clean and dry.

Cool the muffins in the pan for about 10 minutes, then transfer to a wire rack to cool completely. Stored in an airtight container in the refrigerator, the muffins will keep for 1 week.

Spiced Banana Bread with Dried Mango

Bananas, mangoes, and spices all grow on tropical islands, perhaps explaining why they complement each other so well. Here, moist bananas stand in for eggs and give the bread some additional sweetness. Tangy dried mango makes this bread extra special.

Serves 12

INGREDIENTS

1½ cups/195 g whole-wheat pastry flour

½ cup/55 g oat flour

1 tsp baking powder

½ tsp baking soda

¼ tsp salt

1 tsp ground cinnamon

½ tsp ground allspice

¼ tsp ground cloves

1 cup/200 g Sucanat

2 ripe bananas, cut into chunks

½ cup/120 ml nondairy milk

½ cup/120 ml canola oil

2 tbsp ground flaxseeds

1 tsp apple cider vinegar

1 cup/240 g chopped dried mango

METHOD

Preheat the oven to 350°F/180°C/gas 4. Lightly oil a 9-by-5-in/23-by-12-cm loaf pan.

In a large bowl, combine both flours, the baking powder, baking soda, salt, cinnamon, allspice, and cloves and whisk until well mixed.

In a blender, grind the Sucanat until powdery. Add the bananas and blend until smooth. Add the nondairy milk, canola oil, flaxseeds, and vinegar and blend until thoroughly combined. Pour into the flour mixture and stir until just combined. Fold in the mango.

Scrape the batter into the prepared pan and smooth the top. Bake for 50 to 60 minutes, until a toothpick inserted in the center comes out clean and dry.

Cool on a wire rack. Stored tightly wrapped in the refrigerator, the bread will keep for about 1 week.

Using Alternative Flours

For convenience sake, I've tried to keep the flour selections in this book pretty simple, mostly sticking with whole-wheat pastry flour, white whole-wheat flour, whole-wheat flour, and unbleached all-purpose flour. A few recipes call for more unusual flours, like spelt, buckwheat, and oat flour. That doesn't mean that you can't try flours from exciting ancient wheats, like Kamut and farro, or that you can't add a little gluten-free exotica, like quinoa, amaranth, or teff flour. Here are some guidelines on using alternative flours:

- In place of white whole-wheat flour, you can use up to 100 percent spelt or Kamut flour or any flour made from other members of the wheat family.
- For whole-wheat pastry flour, you can substitute up to 50 percent spelt or Kamut flour or any flour made from other members of the wheat family.
- To add some gluten-free flour, replace up to 2 tbsp of each 1 cup/130 g of flour in the recipe with an alternative, gluten-free flour, and see how it turns out. That should be enough to add some flavor, color, texture, or alternative nutrients while still producing baked goods with the structure wheat flour produces.

Peanut Butter and Jelly Banana Bread

If you've ever taken a slice of banana bread, spread some peanut butter on it, and then further embellished it with jam or jelly, this bread is for you. The peanut butter is baked right in, as is the swirl of fruity sweetness, so once it's baked, you don't even have to open any jars.

Serves 12

INGREDIENTS

¼ cup/60 ml nondairy milk

1 tbsp ground flaxseeds

1 cup/130 g whole-wheat pastry flour

1 tsp baking powder

½ tsp baking soda

¼ tsp salt

2 ripe bananas

¾ cup/150 g granular palm sugar, palm sugar paste (see Tip, page 50), or Sucanat

⅓ cup/85 g crunchy peanut butter

2 tbsp canola oil

½ cup/120 ml fruit-sweetened jam

METHOD

Preheat the oven to 350°F/180°C/gas 4. Lightly oil a 9-by-5-in/23-by-12-cm loaf pan.

In a cup or small bowl, whisk the nondairy milk and flaxseeds together and let stand for 5 minutes.

In a large bowl, combine the flour, baking powder, baking soda, and salt and whisk until well mixed.

In a food processor, purée the bananas. Add the sugar, peanut butter, and canola oil and process until smooth. Add the flaxseed mixture and process until thoroughly combined. Pour into the flour mixture and stir until just combined.

Scrape about half of the batter into the prepared pan. Top with half of the jam, dropping it in spoonfuls over the top. Use the back of the spoon to flatten the batter and jam, swirling the jam around just a little. Repeat with the remaining batter and jam.

Bake for 45 to 50 minutes, until golden brown and a toothpick inserted in the center of the loaf (but not in the jam) comes out with moist crumbs attached.

Transfer the pan to a wire rack and let cool completely before removing the bread from the pan and slicing. Stored tightly wrapped in the refrigerator, the bread will keep for about 1 week.

Zucchini Bread with Pecans

The story you hear about zucchini bread is that it was invented to use up the massive harvests of these productive summer squash plants. It may have been, but regardless of its origins, it's a wonderful use for the prolific gourd; moist, mild-flavored zucchini melds beautifully with the sweetness and tender crumb of quick breads.

Serves 12

INGREDIENTS

1 cup/240 ml nondairy milk

2 tbsp ground flaxseeds

2 cups/260 g white whole-wheat flour

¾ cup/150 g Sucanat or granular palm sugar

1 tsp baking powder

1 tsp baking soda

½ tsp salt

¼ cup/60 ml canola oil

1 tbsp apple cider vinegar

1 cup/180 g shredded zucchini

2 tsp arrowroot starch or cornstarch

½ cup/70 g pecans, chopped

METHOD

Preheat the oven to 350°F/180°C/gas 4. Liberally oil a 9-by-5-in/23-by-12-cm loaf pan.

In a cup or small bowl, whisk the nondairy milk and flaxseeds together and let stand for 5 minutes.

In a large bowl, combine the flour, Sucanat, baking powder, baking soda, and salt and whisk until well mixed.

Add the canola oil and vinegar to the flaxseed mixture and stir until thoroughly combined.

In a medium bowl, toss the zucchini with the arrowroot starch until evenly coated.

Pour the flaxseed mixture into the flour mixture and stir until just combined. Fold in the zucchini and pecans.

Scrape the batter into the prepared pan and smooth the top. Bake for about 1 hour, until the top is lightly golden and a toothpick inserted in the center comes out clean and dry.

Cool on a wire rack for 10 minutes, then gently tip the loaf over on its side and let cool completely. Stored tightly wrapped in the refrigerator, the bread will keep for about 1 week.

Holiday Squash Bread with Walnuts

During the winter holidays, it pays to have some tasty quick breads on hand, perhaps even in the freezer, and this one is a great choice. A loaf makes a perfect gift or can provide an easy snack for a hungry crowd of family and friends. You can use pumpkin purée in place of the winter squash and any type of nuts you have on hand; it will still be a really yummy bread.

Serves 12

INGREDIENTS

1 cup/130 g whole-wheat pastry flour

¾ cup/100 g white whole-wheat flour

2 tbsp ground flaxseeds

1 tsp baking soda

½ tsp baking powder

½ tsp salt

2 tsp pumpkin pie spice

1 cup/245 g winter squash purée (see Tip)

1 cup/240 ml maple syrup

½ cup/120 ml canola oil

1 cup/135 g walnuts, chopped

METHOD

Preheat the oven to 350°F/180°C/gas 4. Oil a 9-by-5-in/23-by-12-cm loaf pan.

In a large bowl, combine both flours, the flaxseeds, baking soda, baking powder, salt, and pumpkin pie spice and whisk until well mixed. In a medium bowl, combine the squash purée, maple syrup, and canola oil and whisk until thoroughly blended. Pour into the flour mixture and stir until just combined. Fold in the walnuts.

Scrape the batter into the prepared pan and smooth the top. Bake for about 1 hour, until a toothpick inserted in the center of the loaf comes out with moist crumbs attached.

Cool on a wire rack. Stored tightly wrapped in the refrigerator, the bread will keep for about 1 week.

TIP To make winter squash or pumpkin purée, purchase a winter squash, preferably a variety with drier, denser flesh, like Kabocha, Red Kuri, or Hubbard. Butternut or Acorn will work, too, they are usually just a little moister. Slice the squash in half, scoop out the seeds, place on an oiled sheet. Bake at 400°F/200°C/gas 6 for about 30 minutes, until the squash is tender when pierced with a paring knife. Cool the squash, turning it over to let it release steam, and then scoop the flesh into the food processor bowl and puree. Measure what you need for the recipe and save the rest to mix with maple and spread on scones, or to stir into soups.

FRUIT-BASED DESSERTS, KANTENS & PUDDINGS

There are times when a showcase dessert is absolutely necessary, like a birthday cake or a holiday pie. But if you have a sweet tooth, simpler, more elemental desserts should have a solid place in your repertoire. The desserts in this chapter will fill the bill. They aren't too fancy, but they are plenty tasty. Plus, they're easy to make and generally more nutritious.

However, simple need not be humble, as you'll discover with the fruit-based desserts at the beginning of this chapter. Making fresh, ripe fruits of the season into a satisfying treat is easy with natural sweeteners. Just a few simple moves can take a healthful fruit snack into the realm of company food. The vibrant colors of summer fruits and berries are so beautiful, and their flavors so intense, they practically make dessert for you. Come winter, juicy oranges, sweet grapes, and gorgeous pomegranates and pears can star in special treats that nourish and uplift.

If you have nostalgia for childhood comfort foods, kantens are for you. Kanten, a traditional Japanese dessert, is like gelatin, except that, thankfully, it's made from sea vegetables instead of animal hooves.

Kantens are wonderfully filling, thanks to the fiber in agar, a sea vegetable used to gel them. Unlike gelatin dishes, these treats are made with fruit and fruit juice and don't include a chemistry experiment of artificial colors and flavors.

Aah, comfort me with puddings. Their creamy, spoonable bliss is easy to transform into a vegan treat. The old-school way often meant the double whammy of egg yolks and cream for a super-rich custard, but forget that nonsense. Equally creamy plant-based puddings can be made with silky purées of everything from sweet potatoes to tofu to nuts. Rich coconut milk or nondairy creamer is just as decadent as cream when thickened and flavored for optimum mouth appeal. Baked bread puddings are a great place for those last few slices of whole-wheat bread, soaking up a tasty cream. Frugal, too, since you don't want to waste any of the great bread that you have gone out of your way to find.

Green and Red Grapes in Champagne

If you're looking for a light and simple dessert, this one is both refreshing and elegant. You could just serve fresh fruit, but with a bit of effort you can make a syrup from sparkling wine, then spritz the fruit with more bubbly right before serving. How can you go wrong with fresh fruit that tickles your nose? Feel free to substitute Prosecco, other sparkling wines, or sparkling juice for the champagne.

Serves 4

INGREDIENTS

1½ cups/300 ml champagne

1 tbsp agave syrup

1 cup/150 g seedless red grapes, halved

1 cup/150 g seedless green grapes, halved

4 sprigs fresh mint or rosemary

METHOD

In a small saucepan, bring 1 cup/240 ml of the champagne to a boil over high heat. Lower the heat to medium and cook until reduced to 2 tbsp, about 5 minutes. (Chill the remaining champagne, tightly corked.) Stir in the agave syrup and let stand until cooled a bit.

Add all the grapes to the pan over medium heat, and cook, stirring gently from time to time, until the grapes soften slightly and the red grapes tint the syrup a bit, about 5 minutes. Transfer to a serving dish or storage container, cover tightly, and refrigerate until completely chilled, about 4 hours.

Divide the grapes and their cooking liquid among four wide wine glasses or small glass bowls. Pour 2 tbsp of the remaining champagne over each serving, garnish each with a mint sprig, and serve immediately.

Oranges and Mint in Cinnamon Syrup

A simple bowl of fruit embellished with a few little touches can be a pretty and satisfying dessert. When Cara Cara oranges come in season I love to show them off, but any seedless orange will be wonderful here.

Serves 4

INGREDIENTS

¾ cup/180 ml water

½ cup/120 ml agave syrup

1 stick cinnamon, plus more for garnish (optional)

6 large seedless oranges, preferably Cara Cara

2 tbsp thinly sliced fresh spearmint

METHOD

In a small saucepan, combine the water, agave syrup, and cinnamon. Bring to a boil over high heat. Lower the heat to maintain a low simmer and cook for about 15 minutes, until thick. Let cool to room temperature.

Meanwhile, section the oranges with a sharp knife. Begin by cutting off the stem and blossom ends, slicing all the way down to the juicy pulp. Place the oranges cut-side down and cut off the peel and white pith, again exposing the juicy pulp. Then, working over a medium bowl, cut along each membrane and free the sections, dropping them into the bowl and discarding the membranes. Cover and refrigerate until the syrup is cool.

Pour the syrup over the fruit and scatter the mint over the top. Cover and refrigerate until chilled 4 hours. Spoon the orange segments and syrup into four bowls or glasses and garnish each with a cinnamon stick, if desired, before serving. Stored in an airtight container in the refrigerator, the oranges will keep for about 1 week.

Summer Fruits in Vanilla Syrup

This harkens back to an old-timey picnic, with a fruit jar packed with the ripest summer fruits, simply dressed in syrup. The bonus is that you can keep the fruit suspended in the syrup for a while, and then use the fruit-infused syrup as a special ingredient in lemonade, and mixed drinks and to sweeten every-day foods. Note that you'll need a 1-qt/1-L jar or a deep glass serving dish to show this dessert off to best effect.

Serves 8

INGREDIENTS

1 cup/240 ml white grape juice concentrate

½ cup/120 ml water

¼ cup/60 ml agave syrup

1 vanilla bean

1 cup/155 g sliced fresh peaches

1 cup/130 g fresh raspberries

1 cup/170 g sliced fresh plums

1 cup/155 g fresh blueberries

METHOD

In a medium saucepan, combine the grape juice concentrate, water, agave syrup, and vanilla bean. Bring to a boil over medium heat, then lower the heat and simmer for 5 minutes. Let the syrup cool to room temperature, about 15 minutes.

In a glass jar or serving dish, layer the fruit evenly to show off the contrasting colors. Gently jiggle the jar to compress the fruit. Take the vanilla bean out of the syrup and slide it down inside the jar up against the glass so that it will be visible. Pour the syrup over the fruit and cover tightly.

Refrigerate until well-chilled, about 8 hours, before serving. Stored in an airtight container in the refrigerator, the fruit will keep for about 1 week and leftover syrup will keep for 2 weeks.

Following the Seasons with Fruit

In a world in which produce can travel thousands of miles, you may want to avoid eating fruit that is shipped from another hemisphere. One way to do that is to eat what is local as a first choice, and what's in season as a second choice. Depending on where you live, your seasons may be longer or shorter.

Year-Round	Apples	Bananas	Papayas
	Avocados	Lemons	

Spring	Apricots	Mango	Rhubarb
	Honeydew	Oranges	Strawberries
	Limes	Pineapple	

Summer	Apricots	Figs	Nectarines
	Asian Pear	Grapefruit	Peaches
	Blackberries	Grapes	Plums
	Blueberries	Honeydew	Raspberries
	Cantaloupe	Melons	Strawberries
	Cherries	Mulberries	Watermelon

Fall	Asian Pear	Kumquats	Pineapple
	Cranberries	Pear	Pomegranate
	Grapes	Persimmons	

Winter	Grapefruit	Pear	
	Kiwifruit	Persimmons	
	Oranges	Tangerines	

Figs Stuffed with Almonds in Agave-Orange Syrup

If you don't live in an area where figs grow, getting fresh ones can be hard, even when they're in season. That doesn't mean you have to do without. This recipe showcases dried figs to marvelous effect. Simmered in an orange syrup, they are sticky, sensuous, and infused with the sun-drenched flavors of the Mediterranean. They are delicious over ice cream and also a fun addition to a platter of finger foods. For best results, be sure to use dried figs that are plump and slightly moist.

Serves 4 to 6

INGREDIENTS

1 cup/240 ml water

½ cup/120 ml agave syrup

2 tbsp orange juice concentrate

1 sprig fresh rosemary

12 large dried calimyrna figs

24 whole almonds, lightly toasted (see Tip, page 59)

Slivers of vegan chocolate (optional)

METHOD

In a small saucepan, combine the water, agave syrup, orange juice concentrate, and rosemary. Bring to a boil over medium heat, then lower the heat to maintain to a low simmer.

Carefully snip off the stems of the figs, then stuff two almonds into each fig through the opening, being careful not to tear the figs open. If desired, stuff a sliver of chocolate between the almonds.

Put the figs in the syrup and simmer for 10 to 15 minutes, gently turning the figs a few times to ensure that they are evenly coated with the syrup. When the figs are soft and the remaining syrup in the pan is quite thick but still pourable, transfer the figs to a bowl or jar and pour the syrup over them.

Let cool to room temperature before serving. Stored in an airtight container in the refrigerator, the figs will keep for about 2 weeks.

Dates Stuffed with Walnuts and Dipped in Chocolate

These tasty morsels are great finger food for parties. All-natural and elemental in their appeal, they combine sweetness, crunch, spiciness, and the tingle of mint all in one lush little package.

Serves 3 to 4

INGREDIENTS

12 large Medjool dates with pits

12 large walnut halves, halved lengthwise, plus ¼ cup/30 g walnuts, minced

2 tbsp minced fresh mint

2 tsp agave syrup

¼ tsp coarsely cracked pepper

1½ oz/40 g vegan chocolate, chopped

METHOD

Using a paring knife, cut a slit on the side of each date and pull out the pit, leaving a cavity for the stuffing. In a small bowl, combine the walnuts, mint, agave syrup, and pepper and toss gently until the walnuts are evenly coated. Stuff two pieces of walnut, along with some of the mint and agave syrup, into each date. Close the dates, put them on a plate, and refrigerate.

Melt the chocolate in a double boiler or in the microwave (see Tip), then stir until smooth. Dip each date in the chocolate, cut-side first to seal it closed. Arrange the dipped dates on a serving platter and sprinkle with the minced walnuts before the chocolate sets up.

Refrigerate until the chocolate is completely set, about 2 hours. Let the dates come to room temperature before serving. Stored in an airtight container in the refrigerator, the dates will keep for about 1 week.

TIP If you don't have a double boiler, you can devise one by placing a stainless-steel bowl over a saucepan of simmering water. Choose a bowl that will fit across the top of the saucepan and trap the steam without touching the water.

To melt chocolate in the microwave, put it in a glass measuring cup or bowl and microwave at a low setting, such as 50 percent power, for 1 minute intervals, checking and stirring after each interval. The total time required depends on the quantity of chocolate. If your microwave doesn't have a low setting, use 30-second intervals.

Pomegranate Poached Pears with Cashew Cream

A pear is a lovely thing simply by virtue of its voluptuous form and sweet, mild flesh. In this gorgeous dessert, these natural qualities are enhanced by poaching, the pears in ruby red, antioxidant-rich pomegranate juice and garnishing them with a creamy cashew topping. Feel free to substitute other red or purple juices or red wine for the pomegranate juice. Note that the cashews for the topping should be soaked in advance and that both components of the dessert require several hours of chilling time, so plan ahead.

Serves 4

INGREDIENTS

Poached Pears

4 Bosc pears

2 cups/480 ml pomegranate juice

1 cup/240 ml apple juice concentrate, thawed

¼ cup/60 ml agave syrup

METHOD

To make the poached pears: Carefully peel the pears, leaving the stems on if possible. Using a paring knife, cut a cone-shaped hollow in the base of each pear. Then carefully cut straight up into the pear to remove the seeds and core without cutting through the pear.

Place the pears in a large saucepan and pour in the pomegranate juice, apple juice concentrate, and agave syrup. Bring to a boil over high heat. Lower the heat, partially cover, and simmer for about 20 minutes, turning the pears every 5 minutes to evenly color them and suffuse them with the poaching liquid. Test for doneness by piercing with a paring knife. When the pears are tender but not falling apart, remove from the heat. Use a slotted spoon or tongs to gently transfer them to a plate.

Put the poaching liquid over high heat and bring to a boil. Lower the heat and simmer until reduced to about ½ cup/120 ml, about 10 minutes. The liquid will be quite syrupy, and the bubbles will be large and shiny. Pour the syrup over the pears and baste them with any syrup that pools around them. Refrigerate until well chilled, about 4 hours.

Cashew Cream

1 cup/115 g raw cashews, soaked for at least 2 hours

1 tbsp agave syrup

1 tsp vanilla extract

Pinch of salt

4 tbsp nondairy creamer

4 sprigs fresh mint for garnish

Meanwhile, make the cashew cream: Drain the cashews and pat dry with a clean dish towel. In a blender or food processor, process the cashews until coarsely ground. Add the agave syrup, vanilla, salt, and 2 tbsp of the nondairy creamer and blend until smooth, gradually drizzling in the remaining 2 tbsp nondairy creamer while raising the speed, and stopping a few times to scrape down the sides. Refrigerate until well chilled, about 3 hours.

Serve each pear topped with about ¼ cup/60 ml of the cashew cream; if you like, you can put the cream in a pastry bag with a large star tip and pipe it over the pears for a more decorative presentation. Garnish each serving with a mint sprig.

Sweet Cinnamon Tortillas with Sweet and Fruity Salsa

Chips and salsa are such an easy, friendly food, and this sweet, healthful version has all the charm and none of the drawbacks. These cinnamon-and-Sucanat-sprinkled flour tortillas are great whole-grain dippers for a bowl of colorful fruit spiked with lime juice.

Serves 6

INGREDIENTS

1 tbsp Sucanat

½ tsp ground cinnamon

Six 6-in/15-cm whole-wheat flour tortillas

1½ tsp coconut oil, melted, or canola oil

Sweet Salsa

2 large kiwifruit, peeled and chopped

1½ cups/210 g chopped papaya or mango

1 avocado, diced (optional)

1 tbsp agave syrup

2 tsp fresh lime juice

2 tbsp chopped fresh mint leaves

Vegan sour cream for serving (optional)

METHOD

Preheat the oven to 350°F/180°C/gas 4.

In a blender, combine the Sucanat and cinnamon and grind until powdery.

Put the tortillas on a cutting board in a stack and slice the stack into six wedges. Put the tortillas in a large bowl. Drizzle with the coconut oil and toss to coat. Spread the tortillas on two ungreased baking sheets. Bake for 8 minutes, flipping the tortillas with a metal spatula after 5 minutes of baking.

While the tortillas are hot, hold a small fine-mesh sieve or sifter over them and pour the cinnamon-sugar into it. Shake or sift the cinnamon-sugar over the tortillas, then let cool completely.

Meanwhile, make the salsa: In a medium bowl, combine the kiwi, papaya, and avocado (if using) and stir gently until well mixed. In a cup or small bowl, whisk the agave syrup and lime juice together. Drizzle the mixture over the fruit, then add the mint. Stir gently until well combined.

Serve the chips with the salsa alongside, along with sour cream if you like.

Apple Kanten with Pears

In fall, make this gelled dessert with fresh cider for extra apple flavor. The rest of the year, you can use bottled juice. Feel free to substitute other fruit for the pears, depending on your preferences and what's in season. Just bear in mind that any fruit more acidic than pears will probably require more agar to set well. If using fruits such as oranges, kiwi, mango, and peaches, you'll probably need to increase the amount of agar to 5 or 6 tbsp.

Serves 5

INGREDIENTS

4 cups/960 ml apple juice

¼ cup/10 g agar flakes

1 small cinnamon stick

2 tbsp water

1 tbsp arrowroot starch or cornstarch

¼ tsp vanilla extract

2 ripe pears, sliced

2 tsp fresh lemon juice

METHOD

Combine the apple juice, agar flakes, and cinnamon in a small saucepan. Let stand for 15 minutes, whisking occasionally, to soften the agar. Put the pan over low heat, cover, and slowly bring to a simmer, whisking often until the agar is dissolved; it will take about 10 minutes to begin to bubble.

In a cup or small bowl, whisk the water and arrowroot starch together to form a slurry. Whisk the slurry into the agar mixture and cook, whisking occasionally, until clear and thickened. Whisk in the vanilla. Let cool until just warm.

In a medium bowl, toss the pears with the lemon juice. Transfer to five small serving dishes or a serving dish with a 5-cup/1.2-L capacity.

Pour the mixture over the pears, pressing them down so they remain submerged. Cover and refrigerate until set, about 4 hours. Stored in the refrigerator, tightly covered, the kanten will keep for about 1 week.

Green Tea Kanten with Honeydew

This refreshing kanten is a cool way to enjoy green tea on a summer day. It's also a perfect dish with which to use the intense sweetness of honeydew melons to your advantage. The melon purée sweetens the kanten, which cradles juicy chunks of the green melon, and the remaining honeydew serves as a light and beautiful garnish to serve arranged around it. If you make this dish a day in advance, slice only the half of the melon incorporated into the kanten and wait to slice the remainder until just before serving.

Serves 5

INGREDIENTS

3 cups/720 ml water

4 tsp green tea leaves

¼ cup/60 ml agave syrup

3 tbsp agar flakes

4 lb/8 kg ripe honeydew melon, peeled and cut into spears

2 tbsp water

1 tbsp arrowroot starch or cornstarch

1 cup/125 g fresh berries

METHOD

In a medium saucepan, bring the water to a boil over high heat. Remove from the heat and let cool for about 2 minutes. Add the tea leaves and steep for 4 minutes. Strain the liquid and return it to the saucepan. Add the agave syrup and agar flakes. Let stand for 15 minutes, whisking occasionally, to soften the agar.

Put the pan over low heat, cover, and slowly bring to a simmer, whisking often until the agar is dissolved; it will take about 10 minutes to begin to bubble.

Meanwhile, set aside half of the honeydew spears for garnish and chop the remainder into bite-size pieces. In a blender, purée 1 cup/160 g of the chopped honeydew. Divide the remaining chopped honeydew among five small serving dishes or a serving dish with a 6-cup/1.4-L capacity.

In a cup or small bowl, whisk the water and arrowroot starch together to form a slurry. Whisk the slurry and the honeydew purée into the agar mixture and cook, whisking occasionally, until clear and thickened. Let cool until just warm.

Pour the mixture over the chopped honeydew, pressing the melon down so it remains submerged. Cover and refrigerate until set, about 3 hours.

To serve, surround individual servings of the kanten with the reserved melon slices and about 3 tbsp of the fresh berries. Stored in the refrigerator, tightly covered, the kanten will keep for about 1 week.

Ginger Ale Kanten with Mandarin Oranges

This is the perfect light dessert to follow an Asian-inspired meal. As a bonus, ginger aids in digestion and warms the body, in addition to giving this gelled dessert a spicy tingle on the tongue.

Serves 4

INGREDIENTS

½ cup/120 ml water

¼ cup/10 g agar flakes

1½ cups/360 ml ginger ale

1 cup/240 ml white grape juice concentrate

2 in/5 cm fresh ginger, grated and squeezed to make juice

2 tbsp water

1 tbsp arrowroot starch or cornstarch

15 oz/430 g canned mandarin oranges (packed in water), drained

METHOD

Combine the water and agar flakes in a small saucepan. Let stand for 15 minutes, whisking occasionally, to soften the agar. Add the ginger ale, grape juice concentrate, and ginger juice and whisk until thoroughly blended. Put the pan over low heat, cover, and slowly bring to a simmer, whisking often until the agar is dissolved; it will take about 10 minutes to begin to bubble.

In a cup or small bowl, whisk the water and arrowroot starch together to form a slurry. Whisk the slurry into the agar mixture and cook, whisking occasionally, until clear and thickened. Let cool until just warm.

Put the oranges in four small serving dishes or a serving dish with a 4-cup/960-ml capacity.

Pour the agar mixture over the oranges, pressing them down so they remain submerged. Cover and refrigerate until set, about 4 hours. Stored in the refrigerator, tightly covered, the kanten will keep for about 1 week.

Warm Apple Pudding

If you have apples in the fruit drawer and coconut milk in the pantry, you can make this homey dessert in a snap. You could substitute pears or even mangoes for the apples that top this lush pudding, or even throw some dried fruit in the topping.

Serves 6

INGREDIENTS

2¼ cups/540 ml coconut milk or nondairy creamer

½ cup/100 g Sucanat or granular palm sugar

6 tbsp/45 g arrowroot starch or cornstarch

1 tbsp vanilla extract

⅛ tsp salt

1 tbsp coconut oil or canola oil

4 Granny Smith apples, peeled and cut into ½-inch/12-mm slices

1 tbsp unbleached all-purpose flour

1 tsp fresh lemon juice

1 tsp ground cinnamon

¼ cup/60 ml brown rice syrup

2 tbsp maple syrup

METHOD

Lightly oil a 12-by-8-in/30.5-by-20-cm glass or ceramic baking dish. In a small saucepan, combine 2 cups/480 ml of the coconut milk and the Sucanat. Cook over low heat, whisking frequently, until the Sucanat is dissolved and the mixture is steaming hot but not simmering.

In a cup or small bowl, whisk the remaining ¼ cup/60 ml coconut milk and the arrowroot starch together to form a slurry. Whisk the slurry into the coconut milk mixture, along with the vanilla and salt. Increase the heat to medium and cook, whisking constantly, just until boiling. Pour the mixture into the prepared baking dish.

In a medium frying pan, heat the coconut oil over medium-high heat. Add the apples and sauté until softened but not falling apart, about 10 minutes. Sprinkle with the flour and stir to coat, then sprinkle with the lemon juice and cinnamon and stir to coat. Drizzle in the brown rice syrup and maple syrup and cook, stirring gently on occasion, until the juices are thick and almost cooked away.

Spoon the apples and their cooking liquid evenly over the pudding mixture and let stand at room temperature until the pudding is set, about 1 hour. Serve warm but not hot. Stored in the refrigerator, tightly covered, the pudding will keep for about 1 week.

Cashew-Chocolate Pudding

If you want a truly rich and decadent pudding, try this recipe. Creamy cashew purée has a velvety texture that makes it a perfect stand-in for the dairy and eggs typically used in custards. Be sure to use a good blender for this, or else try a food processor, making sure to grind the cashews until they're perfectly smooth before adding the remaining ingredients. Note that the cashews for the topping should be soaked in advance, so plan ahead.

Serves 8

INGREDIENTS

1 cup/110 g raw cashews, soaked for at least 2 hours

2½ cups/600 ml nondairy milk

¾ cup/150 g granular palm sugar, palm sugar paste (see Tip, page 50), or Sucanat

¼ cup/20 g Dutch-process cocoa powder

¼ cup/30 g arrowroot starch or cornstarch

1 tsp vanilla extract

METHOD

In a blender or food processor, process the cashews until coarsely ground. Gradually add 2 cups/480 ml of the nondairy milk and process until completely smooth. Add the sugar and process until smooth, stopping to scrape down the sides a few times. If the sugar doesn't dissolve, let the mixture stand for 10 minutes, then process again. Add the cocoa powder and process until well mixed.

Pour the mixture into a medium saucepan. Bring to a simmer over low heat. In a cup or small bowl, whisk the remaining ½ cup/120 ml nondairy milk and the arrowroot starch together to form a slurry. Whisk the slurry into the cashew mixture and cook, whisking constantly, until thick, about 5 minutes. Whisk in the vanilla. Transfer to a bowl and cover. Cover and refrigerate until set and completely chilled, about 3 hours. Serve cold. Stored in the refrigerator, tightly covered, the pudding will keep for about 1 week.

Pumpkin-Date Bread Pudding

If you're looking for more ways to enjoy pumpkin, try this recipe. Creamy, rich-tasting pumpkin, coconut milk, and winter spices form a moist, sweet pudding, and tender bread cubes sop up the flavors of this dessert that you might find yourself eating for breakfast the next day. Since it only *seems* decadent, I say, "Why not?"

Serves 8

INGREDIENTS

15 oz/430 g pumpkin purée

1 cup/240 ml coconut milk

½ cup/120 ml agave syrup or maple syrup

2 tbsp arrowroot starch or cornstarch

⅛ tsp salt

2 tsp ground cinnamon

⅛ tsp ground nutmeg

1 tsp vanilla extract

6 cups/ 215 g cubed bread

1 cup/170 g pitted dates, chopped

¼ cup/60 ml brown rice syrup

METHOD

Position two oven racks in the upper and lower third of the oven. Preheat the oven to 350°F/180°C/gas 4. Oil a 12-by-8-in/30.5-by-20 cm glass or ceramic baking dish.

In a large bowl, whisk the pumpkin purée to loosen its texture. Add the coconut milk, agave syrup, arrowroot starch, salt, cinnamon, nutmeg, and vanilla and whisk until thoroughly blended. Fold in the bread cubes and dates and let stand for 5 minutes.

Transfer the mixture to the prepared baking dish and drizzle the brown rice syrup evenly over the top. Bake on the lower rack of the oven for 35 minutes, until a paring knife is hot to the touch after being inserted in the middle of the pudding. Move the pudding to the upper rack and bake for 10 minutes, until the edges are puffed and bubbling and the top is caramelized.

Let cool briefly on a wire rack. Serve warm. Stored in the refrigerator, tightly covered, the pudding will keep for about 1 week.

Chocolate-Orange Bread Pudding

These comforting little pots of pudding are a great way to use up leftover bread. Delicious chocolate and a jolt of orange cover the tofu base, so nobody will be the wiser.

Serves 6

INGREDIENTS

10 oz/280 g silken tofu, drained

1 cup/240 ml nondairy milk

½ cup/120 ml agave syrup

2 tsp vanilla extract

½ cup/40 g Dutch-process cocoa powder

2 tbsp arrowroot starch or cornstarch

¼ tsp salt

6 cups/215 g cubed whole-wheat bread

Grated zest of 1 large orange

METHOD

Preheat the oven to 350°F/180°C/gas 4. Oil six 1-cup/240-ml ramekins.

In a blender or food processor, purée the tofu. Scrape down the sides and process again until completely smooth. Add the nondairy milk, agave syrup, vanilla, cocoa powder, arrowroot starch, and salt and process until smooth.

In a large bowl, toss the bread cubes and orange zest together. Pour the tofu mixture over the bread and stir gently until well combined. Spoon the mixture into the ramekins, dividing it evenly among them and pressing down lightly to get rid of air pockets.

Bake for 30 minutes, until set and browned on top. Let cool before serving, or refrigerate and serve cold. Stored in the refrigerator, tightly covered, the pudding will keep for about 1 week.

CRISPS,
COBBLERS,
PIES &
TARTS

Crisps and cobblers are often referred to as American fruit desserts. Their delicious history starts with European settlers who came to the New World and brought their appetite for sweet treats with them. Because it often wasn't practicable to make the pies and puddings of their homeland, they improvised new desserts using the ingredients at hand, often cooked over an open fire. Necessity was the mother of tasty invention as cooks put seasonal fruits in cast-iron pots and created various biscuit, crumb, and streusel toppings that made the most of the primitive conditions. The resulting desserts are so quick and easy to prepare, not to mention delicious, that they became part of the American home cook's repertoire. We can thank those ingenious cooks for the cobblers and crisps that remain a wonderful way to showcase the best fruit of the season. The simplicity of these desserts also facilitates making vegan versions, free of eggs, dairy, and refined sugar, and healthfully whole-grain to boot.

A little more sophisticated but just as tried-and-true, pies and tarts are easy to put together now that we have things like ovens and countertops. A flaky, tender crust with just a hint of salt and richness cradling a lush, moist filling is one of the most appealing things on Earth. Whether packed with succulent fruit, creamy pudding, or a sweet and crunchy nut filling, pies and tarts just can't be beat.

PB&J Crisp

Everybody loves a peanut butter and jelly sandwich, especially kids. This crisp is a fun and easy take on the familiar lunchbox combo, and it will probably get you more smiles than the sandwich. Now that organic grapes are available most of the year, you can make this crisp in the midwinter for a fresh fruit pick-me-up.

Serves 6

INGREDIENTS

4 cups/600 g red seedless grapes, halved

½ cup/120 ml fruit-sweetened grape jelly

2 tsp arrowroot starch or cornstarch

2 tbsp fresh orange juice

Topping

2 cups/200 g rolled oats

½ cup/65 g whole-wheat pastry flour

½ cup/55 g roasted, unsalted peanuts, chopped

¼ tsp salt

½ cup/100 g granular palm sugar, palm sugar paste (see Tip, page 50), or Sucanat

¼ cup/60 ml coconut oil

¼ cup/65 g crunchy peanut butter

¼ cup/60 ml nondairy milk

METHOD

Preheat the oven to 400°F/200°C/gas 6.

Put the grapes in an ungreased 12-by-8-in/30.5-by-20-cm glass or ceramic baking dish. In a medium bowl, combine the jelly, arrowroot starch, and orange juice and stir vigorously until thoroughly blended. Stir the mixture into the grapes.

To make the topping: In a large bowl, combine the oats, flour, peanuts, and salt and stir until well mixed. In a medium bowl or a food processor, combine the sugar, coconut oil, and peanut butter and mash or process until thoroughly combined. Stir in the nondairy milk. Pour into the oat mixture and stir until well combined. Crumble the mixture over the grapes, distributing it evenly.

Bake for 35 minutes, until the juices are bubbling and the topping is golden and crisp.

Transfer to a wire rack to cool for at least 10 minutes. Serve warm. Stored in the refrigerator, tightly covered, the crisp will keep for about 1 week.

Easy Apple-Pear Crisp with Walnuts

Everybody needs a fallback dessert. This crisp is a perfect one to keep in mind. As long as you have apples and pears on hand, you can whip them together with some pantry staples to make a casserole full of goodness. Vegan Vanilla Ice Cream (page 194) makes a great topping for this dessert, if you can hold back from devouring the crisp long enough to get it out of the freezer.

Serves 6 to 8

INGREDIENTS

2 lb/910 g Granny Smith apples, peeled, cored, and thickly sliced

1½ lb/680 g pears, peeled, cored, and thickly sliced

1 tsp fresh lemon juice

½ tsp vanilla extract

2 tsp arrowroot starch or cornstarch

1 cup/100 g rolled oats

¾ cup/150 g Sucanat or granular palm sugar

½ cup/65 g whole-wheat pastry flour

½ tsp salt

1 tsp ground cinnamon

¼ cup/60 ml walnut or canola oil

¼ cup/60 ml apple juice concentrate, thawed

½ cup/55 g walnuts, coarsely chopped

METHOD

Preheat the oven to 400°F/200°C/gas 6. Lightly oil a 12-by-8-in/30.5-by-20-cm glass or ceramic baking dish.

Put the apples and pears in the prepared baking dish. Sprinkle with the lemon juice, vanilla, and arrowroot starch and toss until the fruit is evenly coated.

In a medium bowl, combine the oats, Sucanat, flour, salt, and cinnamon and stir until well mixed. In a cup or small bowl, stir the walnut oil and apple juice concentrate together. Pour into the oat mixture and stir until well combined. Stir in the walnuts. Scatter the mixture over the fruit, distributing it evenly.

Cover and bake for about 25 minutes, until the juices start to bubble. Uncover and bake for 30 minutes, until the topping is golden brown and the juices are bubbling thickly around the edges.

Transfer to a wire rack to cool for at least 10 minutes. Serve warm. Stored in the refrigerator, tightly covered, the crisp will keep for about 1 week.

Spiced Sweet Potato Bake with Coconut Crumble Topping

If you're looking for a fresh take on sweet potatoes, try this crumble. It's festive enough to include in a holiday dinner, where it will lure all those fans of marshmallow-laced sweet potato casserole away from their sugary old habits. The bonus is that the whole thing is loaded with beneficial fiber and good nutrition, so you can fill folks up while making them happy. Vegan Vanilla Ice Cream (page 194) would be an ideal accompaniment.

Serves 8

INGREDIENTS

1½ lb/680 g sweet potatoes, peeled and cut into ½-in/12-mm cubes

½ cup/120 ml agave syrup

¼ cup/60 ml coconut milk

2 tsp grated lime zest

1 tbsp fresh lime juice

¼ tsp ground allspice

Topping

1 cup/130 g whole-wheat pastry flour

½ cup/50 g rolled oats

½ cup/45 g unsweetened shredded dried coconut

¼ tsp ground ginger

¼ tsp ground nutmeg

Pinch of salt

¾ cup/150 g Sucanat

½ cup/120 ml coconut oil, melted

3 tbsp nondairy milk

½ cup/55 g walnuts, coarsely chopped

METHOD

Position an oven rack in the lower third of the oven. Preheat the oven to 400°F/200°C/gas 6.

In an ungreased 12-by-8-in/30.5-by-20-cm glass or ceramic baking dish, combine the sweet potatoes, agave syrup, coconut milk, lime zest, lime juice, and allspice. Stir gently until well combined. Cover and bake for about 30 minutes, until the sweet potatoes are just tender.

Meanwhile, make the topping: In a large bowl, combine the flour, oats, coconut, ginger, nutmeg, and salt and stir until well mixed. In a blender, grind the Sucanat until powdery, then stir it into the flour mixture. Add the coconut oil and stir until evenly distributed. Sprinkle in the nondairy milk, stir in the walnuts, and mix until thoroughly combined.

Remove the sweet potatoes from the oven and scatter the topping over the top, distributing it evenly. Bake, uncovered, for 30 minutes, until the topping is golden and the juices are bubbling thickly around the edges.

Transfer to a wire rack to cool for at least 10 minutes. Serve warm, Stored in the refrigerator, tightly covered, the crumble will keep for about 1 week.

Nectarine Cobbler with Cinnamon-Swirl Topping

Cobbler is usually a swath of fruit baked with a buttery biscuit topping, but this one has a twist. Instead of freeform biscuits, little cinnamon rolls float on the sweet sea of nectarines, making it like two desserts in one! Just about any juicy fruit makes a good cobbler, so feel free to experiment. But note that you may have to increase the baking time if you use apples.

Serves 8

INGREDIENTS

3 lb/1.4 kg nectarines, pitted and sliced

¾ cup/180 g maple syrup

2 tbsp arrowroot starch or cornstarch

2 tbsp water

2 tsp vanilla extract

Topping

1 cup/130 g whole-wheat pastry flour

½ cup/60 g unbleached all-purpose flour

½ cup/80 g cornmeal

6 tbsp/75 g granular palm sugar, palm sugar paste (see Tip, page 50), or Sucanat

2 tsp baking powder

½ tsp baking soda

¼ tsp salt

¼ cup/60 ml canola oil or light olive oil

½ cup/120 ml nondairy milk

1 tsp ground cinnamon

METHOD

Preheat the oven to 425°F/220°C/gas 7.

In large saucepan, combine the nectarines and maple syrup. In a cup, whisk the arrowroot starch, water, and vanilla together to form a slurry. Stir into the nectarine mixture. Bring to a boil over medium-high heat, then cook, stirring constantly, for about 3 minutes, until it begins to thicken. Transfer to an ungreased 12-by-8-in/30.5-by-20-cm glass or ceramic baking dish.

To make the topping: In a large bowl, combine both flours, the cornmeal, 2 tbsp of the sugar, and the baking powder, baking soda, and salt and whisk until well mixed. In a cup or small bowl, whisk the canola oil and nondairy milk together. Pour into the flour mixture and stir until just combined. Press the mixture together to make a firm dough.

In a small bowl, stir the remaining 4 tbsp/50 g of sugar and the cinnamon together until well mixed.

Transfer the dough to a floured work surface. Shape it into a 10-by-6-in/25-by-15-cm rectangle, gently patting it to an even thickness. Sprinkle the cinnamon-sugar evenly over the dough. Starting at a long edge, roll up the dough to form a long cylinder. Pinch the seam to seal. Place the roll seam-side down and cut it crosswise into 4 even portions, then cut each portion into in 4 slices to make 16 rolls.

Arrange the rolls on top of the nectarine mixture. Bake for 25 minutes, until the rolls are golden brown and the juices are bubbling up around them.

Transfer to a wire rack to cool for at least 10 minutes. Serve warm. Stored in the refrigerator, tightly covered, the cobbler will keep for about 1 week.

Chunky Pumpkin-Pear Pie

The classic pumpkin pie is a smooth and creamy delight, but it isn't vegan-friendly, and you probably have a good vegan recipe already. This celebration of fall combines chunks of pumpkin and pears, bathed in maple syrup. You can use kabocha squash in place of the pumpkin if you like, or apples in place of the pears if you choose sweet ones that bake well.

Serves 8

INGREDIENTS

Filling

3 cups/360 g peeled and finely diced pumpkin

3 cups/330 g peeled and finely diced pears

1 cup/240 ml maple syrup

¼ cup/30 g unbleached all-purpose flour

2 tbsp arrowroot starch or cornstarch

½ tsp ground cinnamon

¼ tsp ground nutmeg

¼ tsp ground ginger

Crust

1½ cups/195 g whole-wheat pastry flour

½ cup/60 g unbleached all-purpose flour

½ tsp salt

¼ cup/60 ml coconut oil, chilled (see Tip)

2 tbsp canola oil

½ cup/120 ml ice water, plus more as needed

½ tsp apple cider vinegar

METHOD

Position an oven rack in the lower third of the oven. Preheat the oven to 425°F/220°C/gas 7.

To make the filling: In a large bowl, combine the pumpkin and pears. In a medium bowl, combine the maple syrup, flour, arrowroot starch, cinnamon, nutmeg, and ginger and whisk until thoroughly blended. Pour over the pumpkin and pears and stir gently until thoroughly combined.

To make the crust: In a large bowl, combine both flours and the salt and whisk until well mixed. Grate the chilled coconut oil into the flour mixture, then toss until the bits of coconut oil are evenly coated. Mix gently with your fingers, squeezing to break up the bits and working quickly so the warmth from your hands doesn't melt the coconut oil. Drizzle in the canola oil while tossing the flour with a fork. In a cup or small bowl, stir the ice water and vinegar together. Drizzle over the flour mixture while still tossing the mixture with a fork, then start mixing with your hands, adding a bit more water if needed to moisten all of the flour. You may need to add 1 to 2 tbsp of water to make a pliable dough. As soon as the dough holds together when pressed, form it into a disk.

Divide the dough into two portions, one slightly larger for the bottom crust. On a lightly floured work surface, roll out the larger piece to form a round with a diameter of about 12 in/30.5 cm. Fit it into a 9-in/23-cm pie pan. Roll out the smaller portion to a round with a diameter slightly smaller than 9 in/23 cm.

Pour the filling into the pie shell, scraping in the last of the juices with a spatula. Top with the second round of dough. Pinch the edges to seal, fluting the edge as you go. Cut four slits and a center hole in the top crust so steam can vent.

Bake for 25 minutes. Lower the heat to 375°F/190°C/gas 5. Put a baking sheet under the pie to catch any juices and cover the pie loosely with foil. Bake for 40 to 50 minutes more. Remove the foil, move the pie to the top rack, and bake for 10 to 15 minutes longer, until the juices are bubbling through the center vent.

Transfer to a wire rack and let cool for at least 1 hour before cutting. Stored in the refrigerator, tightly covered, the pie will keep for about 1 week.

TIP When a recipe calls for chilled coconut oil or melted coconut oil, success depends on using it in that form. Solid oil won't be absorbed by the flour, whereas liquid oil will. This can affect the amount of liquid needed in the recipe, as well as the texture. Here are some tips on using chilled coconut oil: Melt the oil in its jar by placing in a pan of hot water or briefly microwaving it. Pour the amount you need into a glass liquid measuring cup, then refrigerate. When the oil is completely solid, run hot water on the outside of the cup and use a table knife to gently pry the oil out onto a plate. Refrigerate until you're ready to use it. The oil will be quite hard, and when grated, it will form flakes that are just the right size for flaky pastry.

Peach Pie with Streusel

When the brief but glorious season of tree-ripe peaches arrives, eat them fresh until you can't eat any more, then make this pie. The crunchy streusel topping with its hint of cinnamon will affirm just how wonderful it is that peaches are in the world, and in your pie.

Serves 8

INGREDIENTS

Pie Crust

1 cup/130 g whole-wheat pastry flour

½ cup/60 g unbleached all-purpose flour

½ tsp salt

¼ cup/60 ml coconut oil, chilled (see Tip, page 129)

2 tbsp canola oil

¼ cup/60 ml ice water, plus more as needed

METHOD

To make the crust: In a large bowl, combine both flours and the salt and whisk until well mixed. Grate the chilled coconut oil into the flour mixture, then toss until the bits of coconut oil are evenly coated. Mix gently with your fingers, squeezing to break up the bits and working quickly so the warmth from your hands doesn't melt the coconut oil. Drizzle in the canola oil while tossing the mixture with a fork. Drizzle in the ice water, 1 tbsp at a time, while still tossing the mixture with a fork, then start mixing with your hands, adding a bit more water if needed to moisten all of the flour. You may need to add 1 to 2 tbsp of water to make a pliable dough. As soon as the dough holds together when pressed, form it into a disk.

On a lightly floured work surface, roll out the dough to a round with a diameter of about 12 in/30.5 cm. Fit it into a 9-in/23-cm pie pan and flute the edges. Cover and refrigerate for at least 1 hour.

Position an oven rack in the lower third of the oven. Preheat the oven to 400°F/200°C/gas 6.

Continued

Filling

2 lb/910 g fresh peaches, peeled and sliced

1 tbsp fresh lemon juice

1 tsp vanilla extract

1 cup/200 g granular palm sugar or Sucanat

2 tbsp unbleached all-purpose flour

2 tbsp arrowroot starch or cornstarch

Streusel

½ cup/65 g whole-wheat pastry flour

½ cup/100 g granular palm sugar or Sucanat

½ cup/50 g rolled oats

1 tsp ground cinnamon

Pinch of Salt

¼ cup/60ml coconut oil, melted

To make the filling: In a large bowl, combine the peaches, lemon juice, vanilla, sugar, flour, and arrowroot starch and stir gently until thoroughly combined.

To make the streusel: In a medium bowl, combine the flour, sugar, oats, cinnamon, and salt and stir until well mixed. Stir in the coconut oil.

Pour the filling into the pie shell; it will mound up above the rim. Scatter the streusel evenly over the top. Cover loosely with foil.

Bake for 20 minutes. Lower the heat to 375/190°C/gas 5 and put a baking sheet under the pie to catch any juices. Bake for 30 minutes more. Remove the foil and bake for 20 to 30 minutes longer, until the juices are bubbling thickly around the edges and the streusel is browned.

Transfer to a wire rack to cool for at least 40 minutes before cutting. Stored in the refrigerator, tightly covered, the pie will keep for about 1 week.

"Sour Cream" Raisin Pie

Sour cream and raisin pies and bars are classic desserts that make great use of the easy-to-store pantry staple of dried fruit. This version is even easier to make at a moment's notice year-round, since you can keep almost all of the ingredients on hand in the cupboard. Feel free to flout tradition and use dried cherries, cranberries, or even blueberries in place of the raisins if you like.

Serves 8

INGREDIENTS

1 unbaked Pie Crust (page 130), refrigerated for at least 1 hour

12 oz/340 g silken tofu, drained

¾ cup/180 ml agave syrup

¼ cup/60 ml fresh lemon juice

1 tsp vanilla extract

¼ cup/30 g arrowroot starch or cornstarch

¼ tsp salt

½ tsp ground nutmeg

1¾ cups/300 g raisins

METHOD

Preheat the oven to 400°F/200°C/gas 6.

Poke the crust several times with the tines of a fork, then line it with foil and fill with pie weights or dried beans. Bake for 15 minutes. Transfer to a wire rack to cool. Remove the pie weights and foil.

Meanwhile, in a blender or food processor, purée the tofu. Scrape down the sides and process again until completely smooth. Add the agave syrup, lemon juice, vanilla, arrowroot starch, salt, and nutmeg and process until thoroughly blended. Scrape into a large bowl and stir in the raisins.

Scrape the mixture into the pie shell and smooth the top. Bake for 40 minutes, until browned on top and firm to the touch.

Transfer to a wire rack and let cool completely. Cover and refrigerate until completely chilled. Serve cold. Stored in the refrigerator, tightly covered, the pie will keep for about 1 week.

Apple Cider, Date, and Pecan Tart

Pecan pie is typically a super-rich, super-sweet treat, loaded with sugar, butter, and eggs. This version is lighter but just as appealing, with tender, sweet dates and apple cider providing the base for all those crunchy pecans.

Serves 8

INGREDIENTS

Tart Shell

1½ cups/195 g whole-wheat pastry flour

½ tsp salt

6 tbsp/90 ml coconut oil, chilled (see Tip, page 129)

1 tbsp canola oil

¼ cup ice water, plus more as needed

METHOD

To make the tart shell: In a large bowl, combine the flour and salt and whisk until well mixed. Grate the chilled coconut oil into the flour mixture, then toss until the bits of coconut oil are evenly coated. Mix gently with your fingers, squeezing to break up the bits and working quickly so the warmth from your hands doesn't melt the coconut oil. Drizzle in the canola oil while tossing the mixture with a fork. Drizzle in the ice water while still tossing the mixture with a fork, then start mixing with your hands, adding a bit more water if needed to moisten all of the flour; you may need to add up to 1 tbsp more water to make a dough that holds together but isn't too soft. As soon as the dough holds together when pressed, form it into a disk.

On a generously floured work surface, roll out the dough to a round with a diameter of about 13 in/33 cm. It will be delicate, so use a big spatula to transfer it into a 10-in/25-cm tart pan; you may have to piece it together in the pan. Fold in the edges to form a nice rim, even with the edges of the tart pan. Poke in several places with a fork. Refrigerate for at least 1 hour.

Preheat the oven to 400°F/200°C/gas 6.

Line the tart shell with foil and fill with pie weights or dried beans. Bake for 15 minutes. Transfer to a wire rack to cool. Remove the pie weights and foil.

Filling

4½ cups/1 L apple cider, or 1½ cups/360 ml
apple juice concentrate, thawed

½ cup/120 ml maple syrup

2 tbsp bourbon

1 tsp vanilla extract

¼ cup/30 g arrowroot starch or cornstarch

1½ cups/200 g pecan halves

1½ cups/255 g pitted dates, chopped

Meanwhile, make the filling: If using apple cider, put 4 cups/960 ml of the cider in a medium saucepan over medium heat. Cook, stirring occasionally, until reduced to 1½ cups/360 ml, about 20 minutes. Pour ½ cup/120 ml of the reduced cider into a cup or small bowl and set aside. If using apple juice concentrate, set aside ½ cup/120 ml of the concentrate and heat the remainder in a small saucepan.

Add the maple syrup, bourbon, and vanilla to the saucepan and simmer for a few minutes. Whisk the arrowroot starch into the reserved ½ cup/120 ml of cider to form a slurry. Pour into the saucepan and cook, whisking constantly, until thickened.

Spread the pecans and dates in the tart shell. Drizzle the cider mixture evenly over them and use a spoon to gently move them until they are evenly coated and evenly distributed. Bake for 20 to 25 minutes, until the juices are bubbly and very thick.

Transfer to a wire rack and let cool completely before slicing. Stored in the refrigerator, tightly covered, the tart will keep for about 1 week.

Vegan Crusts

Whether you've mastered making conventional pie and tart crusts made with shortening, lard, or butter or are a pie novice and a little intimidated by the crust, don't let that stop you from trying the vegan crusts in this book. Vegan crusts follow many of the same rules as traditional crusts, with a few crucial differences. First is the flour. Nobody wants a tough crust, so I've called for flours that help minimize the formation of gluten. That means using lower-gluten whole-wheat pastry flour, which will yield a more tender crust. But because whole-wheat flour has more bran and germ in it, crusts made with it can be a little crumbly if you go 100 percent, so in some of the recipes in this book I included a bit of unbleached all-purpose flour.

Where whole-grain enthusiasts part ways with regular pastry chefs is when it comes to chilling the dough. It's still important to use ice water and chilled oil, but once the dough is formed into a disk, don't think that chilling it is a good idea, other than just briefly to firm up the coconut oil on a hot day. As pastry dough disks made with white flour sit in the fridge, the cold temperature inhibits gluten formation and makes the solid fats firm again, and this is a good thing. But for some reason, whole-wheat crusts become dry and impossible to roll out with long chilling. That's why these recipes call for only briefly refrigerating the dough, or for rolling out and forming the crust before chilling. A little time in the fridge after shaping relaxes the gluten and makes the shredded coconut oil firm again, which makes for a flakier crust. Be gentle when working with pastry dough, and you should have tender, flaky pastry cradling your delicious pie filling when you are done. The take-home message? Chill the dough and crusts in this book only as long as directed.

Blueberry Tart

Blueberries are all the rage, with their protective bounty of antioxidants naturally packaged in a form that just happens to be sweet and juicy. They deserve the royal treatment they get in this tart, where they bejewel a spread of creamy pastry cream. Feel free to substitute other whole berries; all will shine in this dessert. Mix up the shape of the tart pan you use to fit the occasion. This tart has a lightly sweet crust, adding another dimension of flavor that complements the tart berries.

Serves 8

INGREDIENTS

Tart Shell

1 cup/130 g whole-wheat pastry flour

¼ cup/30 g unbleached all-purpose flour

2 tbsp Sucanat or granular palm sugar

⅛ tsp salt

2 tbsp canola oil

2 tbsp coconut oil, melted

¼ cup/60 ml ice water, plus more as needed

METHOD

To make the tart shell: In a large bowl, combine both flours, the Sucanat, and salt and whisk until well mixed. Drizzle in both oils while tossing the flour with a fork. Drizzle in the ice water, still tossing the mixture with a fork, then start mixing with your hands, adding a bit more water if needed to moisten all of the flour. As soon as the dough holds together when pressed, form it into a disk.

On a lightly floured work surface, roll out the dough to a round with a diameter of about 13 in/33 cm. It will be thin and delicate, so use a big spatula to transfer it into a 10-in/25-cm tart pan with a removable bottom. Trim or fold the edges and patch any tears by pressing the dough back together. Poke the tart shell several times with the tines of a fork, then line it with foil and fill the bottom with pie weights or dried beans. Refrigerate the tart shell while the oven is preheating.

Preheat the oven to 400°F/200°C/gas 6.

Bake the tart shell for 20 minutes, then remove the pie weights and foil and bake for 5 minutes, until crisp and browned. Transfer to a wire rack and let cool completely.

Continued

Pastry Cream

1¾ cups/420 ml nondairy milk

½ cup/120 ml agave syrup

⅛ tsp salt

¼ cup/30 g arrowroot starch or cornstarch

1 tbsp unbleached all-purpose flour

½ cup/120 ml fruit-sweetened apricot jam

1 tsp vanilla extract

2 cups/310 g fresh blueberries

¼ cup/60 ml fruit-sweetened apricot jam

1 tbsp water

Orange zest for garnish (optional)

Meanwhile, make the pastry cream: In a medium saucepan, combine 1 ¼ cups/300 ml of the nondairy milk, the agave syrup, and salt. Bring to a simmer over medium-low heat. In a small cup or bowl, whisk the remaining ½ cup/120 ml of nondairy milk, and the arrowroot starch, and flour together to form a slurry. Pour into the saucepan and cook, whisking constantly, until quite thick. Add the jam and vanilla and stir until thoroughly combined. Scrape the mixture into a bowl. Cover and refrigerate for about 4 hours, until completely chilled.

Spread the pastry cream in the tart shell. Distribute the berries evenly over the top, pressing gently to embed them. Refrigerate until set, about 3 hours.

In a cup or small bowl, whisk the jam and water together, then gently brush the mixture over the berries. Garnish with the orange zest, if desired. Slice and serve chilled. Stored in the refrigerator, tightly covered, the tart will keep for about 1 week.

Raspberry Tart with Cashew Pastry Cream

Creamy cashews make a luscious base for a strewing of ruby berries, all atop a crisp and flaky shell. Other small berries, or even nuggets of dried fruit, could stand in for the raspberries if you are so moved. If you prefer a light-colored cashew cream, be sure to choose a pale sugar; palm sugar paste will make a lighter custard than darker-brown Sucanat. Note that the cashews for the topping should be soaked in advance, so plan ahead.

Serves 8

INGREDIENTS

Tart Shell

3 tbsp Sucanat or granular palm sugar

1 cup/130 g whole-wheat pastry flour

¼ cup/30 g unbleached all-purpose flour

¼ tsp salt

¼ cup/60 ml coconut oil, chilled (see Tip, page 129)

¼ cup/60 ml ice water, plus more as needed

Cashew Pastry Cream

1 cup/115 g raw cashews, soaked for at least 2 hours

½ cup/120 ml nondairy milk

½ cup/100 g palm sugar paste (see Tip, page 50), granular palm sugar, or Sucanat

2 tbsp arrowroot starch or cornstarch

½ tsp vanilla extract

½ tsp almond extract

2 cups/255 g fresh raspberries

METHOD

To make the tart shell: In a blender, grind the Sucanat until powdery. Transfer to a large bowl, add both flours and the salt and whisk until well mixed. Grate the chilled coconut oil into the flour mixture, then toss until the bits of coconut oil are evenly coated. Mix gently with your fingers, squeezing to break up the bits and working quickly so the warmth from your hands doesn't melt the coconut oil. Drizzle in the ice water while tossing the mixture with a fork, then start mixing with your hands, adding more water if needed to moisten all of the flour. You may need to add up to 2 tbsp more water to make a pliable dough. As soon as the dough holds together when pressed, form it into a disk. Wrap tightly in plastic wrap and chill for 20 minutes.

Preheat the oven to 400°F/200°C/gas 6.

On a lightly floured work surface, roll out the dough to a round with a diameter of about 13 in/33 cm. It will be thin and delicate, so use a big spatula to transfer it into a 10-in/25-cm tart pan. Fold the edges under and shape to make a nice rim, even with the edge of the pan. Refrigerate the tart shell while you prepare the pastry cream.

To make the Cashew Pastry Cream: In a blender or food processor, process the cashews until finely ground. With the motor running, drizzle in about half of the nondairy milk and process until smooth. Add the remaining nondairy milk and the sugar, arrowroot starch, vanilla, and almond extract and blend until smooth and thoroughly combined, stopping a few times to scrape down the sides.

Pour the cashew mixture into the tart shell. Sprinkle the raspberries evenly over the top, pressing gently to embed them. Bake for 25 to 30 minutes, until the cashew mixture is set and slightly puffed.

Transfer to a wire rack and let cool completely. Cover and refrigerate until completely chilled. Serve cold. Stored in the refrigerator, tightly covered, the tart will keep for about 1 week.

Rustic Mixed Fruit Tart

The casual drape of crisp pastry filled with a bubbling expanse of sweet fruit makes this dessert "rustic," but don't be deceived by the name—it is very classy. You'll make this simple, fruity tart again and again because it is such a perfect way to show off ripe plums, or any stone fruit, for that matter. Pick an olive oil based on your preferences; you may like a fruity taste, or you may prefer a milder flavor.

Serves 8

INGREDIENTS

Tart Crust

1 cup/130 g whole-wheat pastry flour

½ cup/60 g unbleached all-purpose flour

½ tsp salt

¼ cup/60 ml extra-virgin olive oil

6 tbsp/90 ml ice water, or as needed

¼ tsp apple cider vinegar

Filling

½ cup/100 g Sucanat or granular palm sugar

3 tbsp arrowroot starch or cornstarch

2 lb/910 g plums, sliced

¼ cup/30 g fresh raspberries

Olive oil for brushing

METHOD

Preheat the oven to 400°F/200°C/gas 6.

To make the crust: In a large bowl, combine both flours and the salt and whisk until well mixed. Drizzle in the olive oil while tossing the mixture with a fork. In a cup, stir the ice water and vinegar together. Drizzle in the ice water mixture, while still tossing the mixture with a fork, then start mixing with your hands, adding a bit more water if needed to moisten all of the flour. As soon as the dough holds together when pressed, form it into a disk.

On a lightly floured work surface, roll out the dough to a round with a diameter of 13 to 14 in/33 to 35 cm; it will be very thin. Fold the dough in half and transfer to a baking sheet. Unfold the dough and put it in the refrigerator for 30 minutes. (If you leave it in longer, let it come to room temperature before folding the edges around the filling.)

To make the filling: In a large bowl, combine the Sucanat and arrowroot starch and rub them between your fingers until well mixed. Set aside ¼ cup/60 g of the mixture. Add the plums to the bowl with the remaining Sucanat mixture and stir gently until well combined.

Spread the reserved ¼ cup/60 g of Sucanat mixture evenly over the dough, leaving a 2-in/5-cm border. Top with the plum mixture and fold 3-in/7.5-cm sections of the dough over the fruit. Sprinkle the raspberries over the plums. Lightly brush the dough with olive oil. Cover the entire tart loosely with foil. Bake for 20 minutes. Uncover and bake for 30 minutes more, until the crust is crisp and browned.

Stored in the refrigerator, tightly covered, the tart will keep for about 1 week.

Miniature Caramel-Apple Tarts

As if serving each guest an individual tart isn't special enough, the ruffled phyllo crust gives these four-bite gems a photo-ready look. The components of this festive dessert can be made up to a day in advance—a bonus when entertaining. Just remember that they must be assembled no more than two hours before serving to keep the crust crisp.

Makes 12 mini tarts

INGREDIENTS

Caramel Sauce

½ cup/120 ml brown rice syrup

¼ cup/60 ml maple syrup

1 tsp grated lemon zest

2 tbsp cashew butter

2 tbsp coconut milk

2 tbsp arrowroot starch or cornstarch

1 tsp vanilla extract

⅛ tsp salt

4 tbsp/60 ml coconut oil

2 lb/910 g Granny Smith apples, peeled, cored, and sliced

1 tbsp unbleached all-purpose flour

4 sheets whole-wheat phyllo dough, thawed overnight in the refrigerator

12 lemon zest curls for garnish (see Tip, page 145)

METHOD

To make the caramel sauce: In a small saucepan, combine the brown rice syrup, maple syrup, and lemon zest and whisk until thoroughly blended. While stirring constantly, bring to a boil over medium-high heat. Lower the heat to maintain a low boil and cook for 3 minutes. Remove from the heat and whisk in the cashew butter.

In a cup or small bowl, whisk the coconut milk and arrowroot starch together to form a slurry. Pour into the saucepan. Bring the syrup mixture back to a boil over medium heat and cook, stirring frequently, until thick, about 2 minutes. Remove from the heat and whisk in the vanilla and salt. Let cool to room temperature.

Preheat the oven to 350°F/180°C/gas 4.

In a large frying pan, heat 1 tsp of the coconut oil over medium heat. Add the apples, increase the heat to medium-high, and sauté until the apples are very tender and a few are falling apart, about 5 minutes. Be sure that any excess juices have cooked off; otherwise they will make the pastry soggy. Sprinkle the flour over the apples, stir gently until evenly coated, and cook for 2 minutes. Let cool to room temperature.

Melt the remaining coconut oil. Place a sheet of phyllo on the counter and brush it with some of the oil. Place another sheet of phyllo on top and brush it with oil, and continue in this way with the remaining two sheets. Brush the remaining oil in twelve muffin cups.

Continued

Using a long, sharp knife, cut the stack of phyllo sheets 3 by 4, to make 12 squares. Press each square into a muffin cup, ruffling the edges decoratively. Bake for 10 to 12 minutes, until the phyllo is golden and crisp. Transfer the pan to a wire rack and let cool completely.

No more than 2 hours before serving, assemble the tarts. Combine the caramel sauce and the apples and stir gently until well combined. Scoop the apple mixture into the phyllo cups, distributing it evenly among them. Serve garnished with the lemon zest curls.

(If you won't be serving the tarts all at once, the apple and caramel sauce mixture can be stored in an airtight container in the refrigerator for about 1 day; just bring it back to room temperature and stir well before assembling the tarts. The phyllo shells are best made no more than a few hours before serving, but if need be, they can be stored in an airtight container at room temperature for about 1 week, allowing you to assemble only as many tarts as you need at any given time.)

TIP To make lemon zest curls, use a channel knife to cut strips from a large lemon.

Black-Bottom Chocolate Pudding Tart

Rich, creamy chocolate pies are no longer off-limits for vegans. This wildly delicious version rivals any decadent restaurant dessert made for chocolate lovers. The recipe uses an easy, no-bake crust, but if you prefer, you can make the pie crust on page 130 and bake it blind (as for the "Sour Cream" Raisin Pie on page 133), then fill it with the chocolate filling.

Serves 8

INGREDIENTS

Crust

1 cup/170 g pitted dates

2 tbsp coconut oil

¾ cup/75 g rolled oats

¾ cup/70 g unsweetened shredded dried coconut

2 tbsp Dutch-process cocoa powder

Pinch of salt

1 tbsp nondairy milk, plus more as needed

3 oz/90 g vegan semisweet chocolate, melted

Filling

One 13.5-oz/400-ml can coconut milk, chilled

½ cup/120 ml plus 2 tbsp nondairy milk, or as needed

½ cup/100 g granular palm sugar, palm sugar paste (see Tip, page 50), or Sucanat

½ tsp agar powder

2 tsp arrowroot starch or cornstarch

1 tsp vanilla extract

3 oz/85 g unsweetened chocolate, chopped

METHOD

To make the crust: In a food processor, combine the dates and coconut oil and process until smooth. Add the oats, coconut, cocoa powder, and salt and process until smooth and sticky (bits of chopped oats may still be visible). Add the nondairy milk and pulse to combine. Check to see if the mixture holds together when squeezed. If not, keep pulsing and add a bit more nondairy milk, 1 tsp at a time, until it holds together. Scrape the mixture into the prepared pan. Dampen your fingers and press the mixture into the pan and up to the rim in an even layer. Refrigerate until firm, about 1 hour.

Melt the chocolate in a double boiler or the microwave (see Tip, page 105). Stir until smooth, then carefully spread it over the bottom of the crust. Refrigerate the crust while you prepare the filling.

To make the filling: Turn the can of chilled coconut milk upside down and open the can. Pour off the liquid into a measuring cup. Put the coconut cream back in the refrigerator.

Add nondairy milk to the coconut liquid to bring the level up to 1 cup/240 ml. Pour into a small saucepan and add the sugar and agar powder. Bring to a boil over medium-low heat, whisking constantly, and cook until the sugar and agar powder dissolve.

Continued

In a cup or small bowl, whisk the 2 tbsp nondairy milk and the arrow-root starch together to form a slurry. Pour into the saucepan and cook, whisking constantly, until thickened. Remove from the heat and stir in the vanilla. Add the chocolate and let stand for 1 minute, then whisk until the chocolate has melted and the mixture is smooth.

Pour the mixture into a medium bowl and cover with wax paper, pressing it onto the surface. Refrigerate until completely chilled, about 2 hours. Put a mixing bowl and the beaters of an electric mixer in the freezer.

Stir the filling, keeping an eye out for lumps. If it's lumpy, press it through a fine-mesh sieve.

Working quickly, remove the chilled coconut cream from the refrigerator and the bowl and beaters from the freezer. Scrape the coconut cream into the bowl and beat on high speed until it starts to hold soft peaks, about 3 minutes. Gently fold the whipped coconut cream into the chocolate mixture.

Scrape the filling into the crust and spread it in an even layer. Serve chilled. Stored in the refrigerator, tightly covered, the tart will keep for about 1 week.

Vegan and Fair Trade Chocolate

For chocolate to be vegan, it can't contain any dairy or white sugar that may have been filtered with bone char. But if you are concerned about what your chocolate dollar supports, you may want to take a step beyond vegan and look for Fair Trade and organic chocolates. Most consumers are surprised to learn that much of the cacao grown in West Africa is the product of child and slave labor. Young boys are sold or kidnapped to work on plantations, under terrible conditions. To avoid participating in this, you can seek out Fair Trade and Organic labels on your vegan chocolates.

The good news is that many responsible chocolate makers are making vegan, Fair Trade chocolates. The Fair Trade label promises to use no child labor and means that the farmer was paid a better price. Organic chocolates should be slavery-free, and since organic sugar is not made using bone char, organic dark chocolate should be vegan. The label will let you know if it is made in a factory that also processes dairy. Because the labor problems are largely in West Africa on the Ivory Coast, chocolate that is sourced in other regions of the world is usually not a problem. So, organic chocolate is a good bet, as are chocolates that give their source for beans as Latin America.

There are many reputable sources of information about this issue, and I urge you to be informed about the sources of your chocolate.

COOKIES, BARS, CAKES, CUPCAKES & OTHER SWEET TREATS

Consider the cookie. Even the name is cute, and no matter what form it takes, it's lovable. Whether it's a chunky chocolate chip cookie or a delicate tea nibble, the cookie has a place in just about everyone's heart—and tummy! The same goes for their many cousins, from rich, melty brownies to chewy fruit-filled bars. The conventional versions of these sweet treats are typically loaded with butter, eggs, white sugar, and white flour, which equates to an awful lot of calories without a lot of nutrition. But help is on its way! The cookie and bar recipes in this chapter will ring all the right bells, with whole-foods nutrition hidden in the adorable package. In fact, many of these seemingly decadent treats are more nutritious than the energy bars that people tend to place on a nutritional pedestal.

Of course, we can't do without cakes and cupcakes. They have become identified with birthday parties, and if you doubt it, just take a look at birthday cards on the rack and count how many of them feature a big, fat cake. Going vegan doesn't mean you and your family have to give that up. In fact, the cakes and cupcakes in this chapter can serve as ambassadors for a vegan, whole-foods approach, convincing

even skeptics that you can eat great food without compromising your health. Making tasty vegan cakes isn't as hard as you might think, and once you learn a few new approaches to frosting, you'll be on the road to success.

A tasty goodie need not fall into any standard category of cookie, cake, cobbler, crisp, or what have you. That's certainly the case with the recipes at the end of this chapter. I assure you that your taste buds won't care that it's not quite a tart, pie, or bar once you take a bite.

Lemon and Pine Nut Cookies

In Greece, little cookies like these make the most of the local olive oil, pine nuts, and zingy lemons. Crisp and only mildly sweet, this vegan version is perfect with a cup of tea.

Make about 16 cookies

INGREDIENTS

½ cup/55 g pine nuts

1 cup/130 g whole-wheat pastry flour

½ cup/60 g unbleached all-purpose flour

¼ cup/50 g granular palm sugar or Sucanat

3 tbsp grated lemon zest

¼ tsp baking powder

¼ tsp baking soda

¼ tsp salt

¼ cup/60 ml water, plus more as needed

2 tsp egg replacer, such as Ener-G

¼ cup/60 ml extra-virgin olive oil

METHOD

Preheat the oven to 375°F/190°C/gas 5.

Spread the pine nuts on a rimmed baking sheet and toast for about 5 minutes. Let cool.

Meanwhile, in a large bowl, combine both flours, the sugar, lemon zest, baking powder, baking soda, and salt and whisk until well mixed. In a medium bowl, whisk the ¼ cup/60 ml water and egg replacer together until smooth and frothy, then whisk in the olive oil. Pour into the flour mixture and stir until just mixed. If the dough is too crumbly to hold together, knead in another 1 tbsp of water. Add the toasted pine nuts and knead to combine.

Scoop a 1-tbsp portion of dough and form it into a ball. Place the balls on an ungreased baking sheet, leaving about 2 in/5 cm of space between them. Using wet palms, flatten the balls to a thickness of about ¼ in/6mm.

Bake for 10 to 12 minutes, until golden and crisp around the edges and still a bit soft in the center.

Let cool on the pan for 5 minutes, then transfer to a wire rack to cool completely. Stored in an airtight container at room temperature, the cookies will keep for about 1 week.

Peanut Butter and Raisin Cookies

Sure, the classic peanut butter cookie is a treat, but it's also a great way to eat healthful, high-protein peanut butter. Even better, if you make peanut butter cookies this way, raisins will provide a chewy, tangy counterpoint and add some good-for-you fruit.

Makes about 15 big cookies

INGREDIENTS

2 cups/260 g whole-wheat pastry flour

2 tbsp ground flaxseeds

1 tsp baking soda

½ tsp salt

1 cup/250 g crunchy peanut butter

1 cup/250 ml brown rice syrup

½ cup/120 ml canola oil

1½ tsp vanilla extract

Nondairy milk, as needed

½ cup/85 g raisins

METHOD

Preheat the oven to 350°F/180°C/gas 4. Line two baking sheets with parchment paper or oil them lightly.

In a large bowl, combine the flour, flaxseeds, baking soda, and salt and whisk until well mixed.

In a food processor, combine the peanut butter, brown rice syrup, canola oil, and vanilla and process until thoroughly combined; alternatively, you can combine the ingredients in a medium bowl and stir by hand (but if the peanut butter is very hard, a food processor will blend the mixture much more easily). Pour the peanut butter mixture into the flour mixture and stir until thoroughly combined. If the dough is too crumbly to hold together, stir in a bit of nondairy milk, 1 tbsp at a time. Knead in the raisins.

Scoop a scant ¼-cup/60-ml portion of dough (oiling the measuring cup makes it easier to remove the dough) and form it into a ball. Place the balls on the prepared baking sheets, leaving about 3 in/7.5 cm of space between them. Using wet palms, flatten the balls to a thickness of about ¾ in/2 cm. If desired, press the tops with the tines of a fork to make the classic crosshatch marks.

Bake for 20 to 22 minutes, until the edges are golden and the cookies are puffed, rotating the pans halfway through the cooking time.

Let cool on the pans for about 5 minutes, then transfer to wire racks to cool completely. Stored in an airtight container at room temperature, the cookies will keep for about 1 week.

Barley-Almond Cookies

Oats are great, but barley is actually higher in beta-glucans, a magical type of soluble fiber that lowers cholesterol. Barley has a lovely, nutty flavor and gives these cookies a pleasant chewiness. If you don't have barley flakes on hand, you can certainly substitute rolled oats. Likewise, you can substitute whole-wheat pastry flour for the barley flour.

Makes about 10 big cookies

INGREDIENTS

2 cups/260 g barley flour

1 cup/100 g barley flakes

½ tsp baking soda

¼ tsp salt

1 tsp ground cinnamon

¼ tsp ground cloves

¾ cup/180 ml maple syrup

¼ cup/60 ml coconut oil, melted

2 tbsp canola or walnut oil

1 tsp vanilla extract

¼ tsp almond extract (optional)

½ cup/70 g raw almonds, coarsely chopped

½ cup/85 g raisins

METHOD

Preheat the oven to 350°F/180°C/gas 4. Lightly oil a baking sheet.

In a large bowl, combine the barley flour, barley flakes, baking soda, salt, cinnamon, and cloves and stir until well mixed. In a medium bowl, combine the maple syrup, coconut oil, canola oil, vanilla, and almond extract (if using) and whisk until thoroughly blended. Pour into the flour mixture and stir until well combined. Fold in the almonds and raisins.

Scoop a ¼-cup/60-ml portion of dough (oiling the measuring cup makes it easier to remove the dough) and form it into a ball. Place the balls on the prepared baking sheet, leaving about 2 in/5 cm of space between them. Using wet palms, flatten the cookies to a thickness of about ¾ in/2 cm.

Bake for about 16 minutes, until lightly golden, rotating the pan halfway through the baking time.

Let cool on the pan for 5 minutes, then transfer to a wire rack to cool completely. Stored in an airtight container at room temperature, the cookies will keep for about 1 week.

Coconut, Almond, and Chocolate Chip Cookies

There is something about the texture of coconut in a cookie; the way it stays moist and chewy is irresistible. The addition of chocolate and almonds makes for a triple temptation that will call to you from the cookie jar.

Makes about 8 big cookies

INGREDIENTS

2 tbsp nondairy milk, plus more as needed

1 tbsp ground flaxseeds

½ cup/60 g unbleached all-purpose flour

½ cup/65 g whole-wheat pastry flour

1 tbsp nutritional yeast (optional)

½ tsp baking soda

¼ tsp salt

½ cup/120 ml canola oil

½ cup/100 g granular palm sugar, palm sugar paste (see Tip, page 50), or Sucanat

½ tsp almond extract

1 cup/90 g unsweetened shredded dried coconut

½ cup/55 g sliced almonds

½ cup/85 g vegan chocolate chips

METHOD

Preheat the oven to 375°F/190°C/gas 5.

In a cup or small bowl, whisk the 2 tbsp nondairy milk and the flaxseeds together and let stand for 5 minutes.

In a large bowl, combine both flours, the nutritional yeast (if using), baking soda, and salt and whisk until well mixed.

In a food processor, combine the canola oil and sugar and process until smooth. Add the almond extract and pulse to combine. Add the flaxseed mixture and process until thoroughly combined. Pour into the flour mixture and stir until just combined. Fold in the coconut, almonds and chocolate chips. If the dough is too crumbly to hold together, knead in up to 2 tbsp more nondairy milk.

Scoop a ¼-cup/60-ml portion of dough (oiling the measuring cup makes it easier to remove the dough) and form it into a ball. Place the balls on an ungreased baking sheet, leaving about 2 in/5 cm of space between them. Using wet palms, flatten slightly to a thickness of just over ½ in/12mm.

Bake for about 16 minutes, until the cookies are quite golden around the edges, rotating the pan halfway through the baking time.

Let cool on the pan for 5 minutes, then transfer to a wire rack to cool completely. Stored in an airtight container at room temperature, the cookies will keep for about 1 week.

Orange and Dried Plum Bars with Walnut Topping

A few years back, there was a trend toward relabeling prunes as "dried plums," perhaps in an attempt to shed the stodgy image that prunes seemed to have. Call them what you will, dried plums give these chewy, crunchy bars a sweet-tart flavor that can't be matched.

Makes 16 bars

INGREDIENTS

Dried Plum Filling

1 lb/455 g pitted dried plums (prunes)

½ cup/120 ml water

½ cup/120 ml agave syrup

3 tbsp orange liqueur

5 tbsp/35 g unbleached all-purpose flour

Crust

1½ cups/195 g whole-wheat pastry flour

½ cup/100 g Sucanat or granular palm sugar

¼ tsp salt

6 tbsp/90 ml coconut oil, chilled (see Tip, page 129)

3 tbsp nondairy milk, plus more as needed

METHOD

To make the plum filling: In a small saucepan, combine the dried plums, water, agave syrup, and orange liqueur. Bring to a boil over high heat, then lower the heat as much as possible, cover, and simmer for 5 minutes. Remove from the heat and let stand for 10 minutes. Sprinkle in the flour and stir until thoroughly combined.

Preheat the oven to 350°F/180°C/gas 4. Oil a 9-in/23-cm square baking pan.

To make the crust: In a medium bowl, combine the pastry flour, Sucanat, and salt and stir until well mixed. Grate the chilled coconut oil into the flour mixture, then toss until the bits of coconut oil are evenly coated. Mix gently with your fingers, squeezing to break up the bits and working quickly so the warmth from your hands doesn't melt the coconut oil. Add the nondairy milk and stir until just combined. Press a bit of the mixture in your hand to see if it holds together; if it's crumbly, stir in a bit more nondairy milk.

Scrape the dough into the prepared pan and press it in an even layer. Bake for 5 minutes. Let cool. Leave the oven on.

Streusel

½ cup/65 g whole-wheat pastry flour

½ cup/50 g rolled oats

½ cup/55 g walnuts, chopped

¼ cup/50 g Sucanat or granular palm sugar

⅛ tsp salt

¼ cup/60 ml coconut oil, melted, plus more as needed

Meanwhile, prepare the streusel: In a medium bowl, combine the flour, oats, walnuts, Sucanat, and salt and stir until well mixed. Add the coconut oil and stir until thoroughly combined. If any loose flour remains, stir in a bit more oil.

Spread the plum filling over the crust in an even layer. Scatter the streusel evenly over the top and press to flatten slightly. Bake for 40 to 45 minutes, until the streusel is golden brown and feels firm to the touch.

Transfer the pan to a wire rack and let cool completely. Cut 4 by 4, to make 16 squares. Stored in an airtight container in the refrigerator, the bars will keep for about 1 week.

Pistachio Brownies with Ganache Topping

Do you love fudgy, gooey brownies, dense with dark chocolate? If so, this recipe will knock your socks off. In fact, it may be too chocolaty for small children. That just means more for you! Feel free to use other nuts in place of pistachios, like the classic walnuts or pecans.

Makes 16 brownies

INGREDIENTS

2 cups/200 g Sucanat

¾ cup/180 ml coconut milk

½ cup/85 g pitted dates

¼ cup/30 g arrowroot starch or cornstarch

2 tbsp ground flaxseeds

1 tsp vanilla extract

½ tsp apple cider vinegar

¾ cup/180 ml coconut oil

3 oz/85 g unsweetened chocolate

1 cup/130 g whole-wheat pastry flour

½ cup/60 g unbleached all-purpose flour

2 tbsp Dutch-process cocoa powder

1 tbsp baking soda

1 tsp baking powder

½ tsp salt

½ cup/55 g toasted pistachios, coarsely chopped

Ganache Topping

½ cup/100 g granular palm sugar, palm sugar paste (see Tip, page 50), or Sucanat

¼ cup/60 ml coconut milk

2 oz/55 g unsweetened chocolate, chopped

METHOD

Preheat the oven to 350°F/180°C/gas 4. Oil a 9-in/23-cm square baking pan.

In a blender, grind the Sucanat until powdery. Add the coconut milk, dates, arrowroot starch, flaxseeds, vanilla, and vinegar and blend until smooth and thoroughly combined.

In a double boiler, combine the coconut oil and chocolate and cook, stirring every few minutes, until melted (see Tip, page 105). Pour into the blender with the Sucanat mixture and blend until smooth and thoroughly combined.

In a large bowl, combine both flours, the cocoa powder, baking soda, baking powder, and salt and whisk until well mixed. Pour in the chocolate mixture and stir until thoroughly combined.

Scrape the batter into the prepared pan and spread it in an even layer. Sprinkle the pistachios evenly over the top, then gently press them into the batter. Bake for about 25 minutes, until the middle is puffy but still soft.

Transfer to a wire rack and let cool completely. Cover and refrigerate until completely chilled, about 2 hours. The brownies will fall and have chewy, higher edges.

Meanwhile, make the topping: In a small saucepan, combine the sugar and coconut milk. Cook over medium-low heat, stirring constantly, until the sugar dissolves. Stir in the chocolate and remove from the heat. Stir until the chocolate has melted and the mixture is smooth.

Drizzle the ganache over the brownies. Cover and refrigerate until the ganache sets up, about 30 minutes. Cut 4 by 4, to make 16 squares. Serve at room temperature. Stored in an airtight container in the refrigerator, the brownies will keep for about 1 week.

Cashew Blondies

In these chewy bars, the caramel notes of both brown rice syrup and palm sugar paste will convince your taste buds that you're eating butter, and the crunchy cashews only add to the sensation—not a bad trick! The sprinkling of coarse salt may seem kind of trendy, but it really brings out the sweetness, so give it a try. If you must gild the lily, a melted dark chocolate drizzle would take these over the top. In a pinch, you could substitute peanuts for the cashews.

Makes 12 bars

INGREDIENTS

¼ cup/60 ml nondairy milk

2 tbsp ground flaxseeds

2 cups/260 g whole-wheat pastry flour

½ tsp salt

¼ tsp baking soda

½ cup/100 g palm sugar paste (see Tip, page 50), granular palm sugar, or Sucanat

½ cup/120 ml coconut oil, melted

½ cup/120 ml brown rice syrup

1 tsp rice vinegar

1 tsp vanilla extract

¾ cup/85 g cashews, toasted (see Tip, page 59) and coarsely chopped

Kosher salt for sprinkling

METHOD

Preheat the oven to 350°F/180°C/gas 4. Line a 13-by-9-in/33-by-23-cm baking pan with parchment paper and oil the parchment paper.

In a cup or small bowl, whisk the nondairy milk and flaxseeds together and let stand for 5 minutes.

In a large bowl, combine the pastry flour, salt, and baking soda and whisk until well mixed. In a medium bowl (or a food processor if the palm sugar is lumpy), combine the palm sugar, coconut oil, and brown rice syrup and stir (or process) until smooth and thoroughly combined.

Stir the vinegar and vanilla into the flaxseed mixture. Add to the sugar mixture and stir (or process) until well combined. Pour into the flour mixture.

Scrape the batter into the prepared pan and spread it in an even layer. Sprinkle the cashews evenly over the top, then gently press them into the batter. Bake for 25 minutes, until the edges are golden and the center looks dry. While still hot, sprinkle a few pinches of kosher salt evenly over the top.

Transfer the pan to a wire rack and let cool completely. Cut 4 by 3, to make 12 squares. Stored at room temperature, tightly covered, the blondies will keep for about 1 week.

Apple Snack Cake

If you keep some applesauce in the cupboard and some apples in the fruit drawer of your refrigerator, you can put this cake together in no time at all. Kids and adults alike are drawn to the decorative shingling of apple slices across the top, and they will want a piece after school or with coffee, or just for fun.

Serves 9

INGREDIENTS

¾ cup/180 ml applesauce

1 cup/130 g whole-wheat pastry flour

1 cup/130 g white whole-wheat flour

1 tsp baking powder

1 tsp baking soda

½ tsp salt

1 tbsp ground cinnamon

1¼ cups/250 g Sucanat or granular palm sugar

2 tsp egg replacer, such as Ener-G

2 tbsp ground flaxseeds

½ cup/120 ml nondairy milk

½ cup/120 ml canola oil

2 tsp vanilla extract

1 tbsp fresh lemon juice, plus 1 tsp

2 large tart apples, peeled, cored, and sliced

METHOD

Preheat the oven to 350°F/180°C/gas 4. Lightly oil a 9-in/23-cm square baking pan.

Fold a clean smooth dish towel in half, then spread the applesauce on it in a thin layer. The towel will absorb a great deal of water from the applesauce in the time it takes to mix the other ingredients.

In a large bowl, combine both flours, the baking powder, baking soda, salt, and cinnamon and whisk until well mixed.

In a food processor, grind the Sucanat as finely as possible. Set aside ¼ cup/60 g and add the remainder to the flour mixture. Mix well.

Put the egg replacer and flaxseeds in a medium bowl and slowly whisk in the nondairy milk. Add the canola oil and vanilla and the 1 tbsp lemon juice.

Use a spatula to scrape the applesauce from the towel and into a measuring cup. It should measure about ½ cup/120 ml. (If it is less, top it off with some plain applesauce; if it is more, just use ½ cup.) Stir the applesauce into the nondairy milk mixture. Pour into the flour mixture and stir until thoroughly combined.

Scrape the batter into the prepared pan. Toss the apple slices with the 1 tsp lemon juice, then arrange them in slightly overlapping rows atop the batter. Sprinkle the reserved ¼ cup/60 g finely ground Sucanat evenly over the top. Bake for about 50 minutes, until a toothpick inserted in the center comes out clean and dry.

Transfer the pan to a wire rack. Let cool completely before cutting. Stored in the refrigerator, tightly covered, the cake will keep for about 1 week.

Pear and Maple Upside-Down Cake

Pineapple upside-down cake is a classic, but why not use local fruit and make this elegant rendition, which uses the natural shape of pears to create a beautiful and supremely edible design? You can also try making this with quartered apples, which will stay firm and hold their shape well.

Serves 12

INGREDIENTS

½ cup/120 ml nondairy milk

2 tbsp ground flaxseeds

1½ cups/195 g whole-wheat pastry flour

½ cup/60 g unbleached all-purpose flour

½ tsp baking powder

½ tsp baking soda

½ tsp salt

½ cup/100 g palm sugar paste (see Tip, page 50), granular palm sugar, or Sucanat

4 small pears, peeled, halved, and cored

½ cup/120 ml maple syrup

¼ cup/60 ml canola oil

½ tsp vanilla extract

½ tsp apple cider vinegar

METHOD

Preheat the oven to 350°F/180°C/gas 4. Oil a 9-in/23-cm cake pan.

In medium bowl, whisk the nondairy milk and flaxseeds together and let stand for 5 minutes.

In a large bowl, combine both flours, the baking powder, baking soda, and salt and whisk until well mixed.

Sprinkle the sugar evenly over the bottom of the prepared pan. Arrange the pears over the sugar, cut-side down and with the wide ends facing out and the pointed tops toward the center, like the spokes of a wheel.

Add the maple syrup, canola oil, vanilla, and vinegar to the flaxseed mixture and whisk until thoroughly blended. Pour into the flour mixture and stir until just combined.

Pour the batter over the pears, being sure to cover all of the pears; it won't seem like quite enough batter, but it will flow out and fill in the spaces. Bake for 40 minutes, until the cake is puffed and golden and a toothpick inserted in the center comes out clean.

Transfer the pan to a wire rack to cool for 5 minutes. Run a table knife around the edges to loosen the cake, then cover the pan with an inverted serving plate. Using oven mitts, hold the pan tight to the plate and invert. Carefully lift off the pan and use the table knife to loosen any pieces of pear or cake stuck to the pan and put them back on the cake. Use a spatula to scrape any caramel-like syrup from the pan and drizzle it over the cake.

Let cool for at least 20 minutes before slicing and serving. Stored in the refrigerator, tightly covered, the cake will keep for about 1 week.

Cinnamon-Crunch-Stuffed Bundt Cake

Who doesn't love a Bundt cake? In this banana-laced version, the unique flavor of palm sugar makes the cinnamon-spiced pecan filling absolutely crave-worthy. The cinnamon drizzle is optional but highly recommended for gilding this wonderful cake with more sweet cinnamon.

Serves 8

INGREDIENTS

1 cup/200 g granular palm sugar, palm sugar paste (see Tip, page 50), or Sucanat

1 tbsp ground cinnamon

½ cup/70 g pecans, chopped

1½ cups/195 g whole-wheat pastry flour

½ cup/60 g unbleached all-purpose flour

1 tsp baking soda

1 tsp baking powder

¼ tsp salt

¾ cup/180 ml mashed bananas

¾ cup/180 ml nondairy milk

½ cup/120 ml canola oil

1 tbsp egg replacer, such as Ener-G

METHOD

Preheat the oven to 350°F/180°C/gas 4. Oil a Bundt pan.

In a small bowl, combine ½ cup/100 g of the sugar and the cinnamon and stir until well mixed. Stir in the pecans.

In a large bowl, combine both flours, the baking soda, baking powder, and salt and whisk until well mixed.

In a food processor, combine the bananas and remaining ½ cup/100 g sugar and process until smooth. Add the nondairy milk, canola oil, and egg replacer and process until smooth and frothy. Pour into the flour mixture and stir until just combined.

Pour half of the batter into the prepared pan and spread it evenly. Sprinkle the pecan mixture in a line down the center of the batter, then push it into the batter lightly to make a tunnel of pecan streusel. Pour in the remaining batter. Spread it in an even layer and smooth with a spatula. Bake for about 45 minutes, until the top is golden brown and a toothpick inserted in the center comes out with moist crumbs attached.

Cool in the pan for 10 minutes. Run a table knife around the edges (both inner and outer) to loosen the cake, then cover the pan with an inverted cake plate. Using oven mitts, hold the pan tight to the plate and invert to drop the cake onto the plate. Let cool completely.

Continued

Cinnamon Drizzle (optional)

2 tbsp agave syrup

½ tsp ground cinnamon

Meanwhile, make the cinnamon drizzle (if desired): In a cup or small bowl, stir the agave syrup and cinnamon together.

Drizzle the mixture over the cake. Stored in the refrigerator, tightly covered, the cake will keep for about 1 week.

Carrot-Orange Cake with Marmalade Glaze

This moist and lovely carrot cake is graced with the flavor of maple syrup and studded with juicy raisins. Instead of the usual creamy frosting, it's topped with a tangy, fruity glaze decorated with canned mandarin oranges. They sparkle like jewels, calling everyone to have a piece.

Serves 12

INGREDIENTS

2½ cups/325 g whole-wheat pastry flour

¼ cup/50 g Sucanat or granular palm sugar

1 tbsp grated orange zest

1 tsp baking powder

1 tsp baking soda

½ tsp salt

1 tsp ground cinnamon

¾ cup/180 ml nondairy milk

2 tsp egg replacer, such as Ener-G

¾ cup/180 ml maple syrup

½ cup/120 ml canola oil

2 cups/220 g grated carrots

1 cup/170 g raisins

METHOD

Preheat the oven to 350°F/180°C/gas 4. Oil a 10-in/25-cm springform pan.

In a large bowl, combine the flour, Sucanat, orange zest, baking powder, baking soda, salt, and cinnamon and whisk until well mixed. In a medium bowl, whisk the nondairy milk and egg replacer together until smooth and frothy. Whisk in the maple syrup and canola oil. Pour into the flour mixture and stir until just combined. Fold in the carrots and raisins.

Scrape the batter into the prepared pan and spread it in an even layer. Bake for 1 hour, until the cake pulls away from the sides of the pan and a toothpick inserted in the center comes out clean and dry.

Transfer the pan to a wire rack and let cool completely. Run a table knife around the edges to loosen the cake. Remove the sides of the spring-form pan and place the cake, still on the bottom of the springform pan, on a cake plate.

Continued

Glaze

¼ cup/60 ml orange juice concentrate

3 tbsp agave syrup

1 tbsp arrowroot starch or cornstarch

½ cup/120 ml fruit sweetened marmalade

10 oz/280 g canned mandarin oranges (packed in water), drained and patted dry

Meanwhile, make the glaze: In a small saucepan, combine the orange juice concentrate, agave syrup, and arrowroot starch and whisk until smooth and thoroughly combined. Whisk in the marmalade, then put the pan over medium heat and cook, whisking frequently, until the mixture boils and thickens, about 5 minutes. Remove from the heat and let cool to room temperature.

Put 3 tbsp of the glaze in a bowl, add the mandarin oranges, and stir gently until evenly coated. Spread the remainder of the glaze over the cake and refrigerate until set, about 1 hour. Arrange the orange sections on top of the cake and refrigerate again.

Serve chilled. Stored in the refrigerator, tightly covered, the cake will keep for about 1 week.

Yellow Cake with Ice Cream Filling and Ganache Glaze

This recipe features the chocolaty goodness of ganache, but the cake is also delicious with Peanut Butter Frosting (page 176) or Cashew Frosting (page 184), so consider it an all-around basic cake that works and plays well with others. I include a bit of nutritional yeast for its golden color and cheesy taste, but you can leave it out if you like.

Serves 8 to 12

INGREDIENTS

1½ cups/195 g whole-wheat pastry flour

½ cup/60 g unbleached all-purpose flour

2 tbsp nutritional yeast (optional)

1 tsp baking soda

½ tsp salt

½ cup/120 ml nondairy milk

2 tsp egg replacer, such as Ener-G

⅔ cup/165 ml agave syrup

½ cup/120 ml coconut oil, melted

1 tbsp apple cider vinegar

2½ cups vegan Vanilla Ice Cream (page 194) or store-bought

Ganache Topping (page 162), warm

Strawberries for garnish (optional)

METHOD

Preheat the oven to 350°F/180°C/gas 4. Oil a 9-in/23-cm cake pan and line the bottom with parchment paper.

In a large bowl, combine both flours, the nutritional yeast (if using), baking soda, and salt and whisk until well mixed. In a medium bowl, whisk the nondairy milk and egg replacer together until smooth and frothy. Whisk in the agave syrup, coconut oil, and vinegar. Pour into the flour mixture and stir vigorously until smooth.

Scrape the batter into the prepared pan and smooth the top. Bake for 25 to 30 minutes, until the cake starts to pull away from the sides of the pan and a toothpick inserted into the center comes out clean and dry.

Transfer the pan to a wire rack and let cool completely. Run a table knife around the edges to loosen the cake, then cover the pan with an inverted plate. Hold the pan tight to the plate and invert, then place another inverted plate atop the cake and invert again. Refrigerate until completely chilled.

About 20 minutes before assembling the cake, remove the ice cream from the freezer to soften and become spreadable.

Using a long serrated knife, split the cake into two layers. Spread the ice cream evenly over the bottom layer of cake, making sure the thickness is even all the way to the edge. Top with the remaining layer of cake and gently press so it adheres to the ice cream. Freeze until completely set, about 2 hours.

Drizzle the warm ganache over the frozen cake, then freeze again until the chocolate is set.

Remove from the freezer about 10 minutes before slicing and serving. Garnish with strawberries, if you like. Stored in the freezer, tightly wrapped or in an airtight container, the cake will keep for about 1 month.

Chocolate Layer Cake with Peanut Butter Frosting

Chocolate cake is always a favorite, and topping it with a creamy coat of peanut-buttery goodness only improves the situation. Who needs butter when we have peanut butter?

Serves 12

INGREDIENTS

Peanut Butter Frosting

9 oz/255 g silken tofu, drained and pressed (see Tip, page 188)

1 cup/250 g smooth peanut butter, not freshly ground

¼ cup/30 g coconut flour or vegan protein powder

¾ cup/180 ml agave syrup or maple syrup

2 tbsp fresh lemon juice

1 tsp vanilla extract

METHOD

To make the frosting: In a blender or food processor, purée the tofu. Scrape down the sides and process again until completely smooth. Add the peanut butter and process until very smooth. Add the coconut flour and process until smooth. Add the agave syrup, lemon juice, and vanilla and process until thoroughly combined. Scrape the frosting into a bowl or storage container, cover, and refrigerate for at least 2 hours.

To make the cake: Preheat the oven to 350°F/180°C/gas 4. Oil two 9-in/23-cm cake pans.

In a large bowl, combine the flour, cocoa powder, baking powder, baking soda, and salt and whisk until well mixed.

In a double boiler, combine the coconut oil and chocolate and cook, stirring every few minutes, until melted (see Tip, page 105). Whisk in the maple syrup.

In a cup or small bowl, whisk the nondairy milk, egg replacer, and flaxseeds together until smooth and frothy. Stir in the vinegar and vanilla, then pour into the chocolate mixture and stir until thoroughly combined. Pour into the flour mixture and stir until well combined.

Cake

2 cups/260 g white whole-wheat flour

¼ cup/20 g Dutch-process cocoa powder

1½ tsp baking powder

1 tsp baking soda

½ tsp salt

½ cup/120 ml coconut oil

2 oz/55 g unsweetened baking chocolate, chopped

¾ cup/180 ml maple syrup

1 cup/240 ml nondairy milk

1 tbsp egg replacer, such as Ener-G

1 tbsp ground flaxseeds

2 tsp rice vinegar

1 tsp vanilla extract

½ cup/55 g roasted, unsalted peanuts, coarsely chopped

Scrape the batter into the prepared pans and smooth the tops. Bake for 20 to 25 minutes, until a toothpick inserted in the center comes out with moist crumbs attached.

Transfer the pans to a wire rack to cool for about 15 minutes. Run a table knife around the edges to loosen the cakes, then cover each pan with an inverted cooling rack or a plate. Invert and remove the pans. Place the final serving plate over one of the cakes and invert to place it on the serving plate.

Cool the cakes completely or wrap and chill before frosting. Spread about one-fourth of the frosting on top of the cake layer on the serving plate. Sprinkle half of the peanuts evenly over the frosting. Carefully place the second layer on top, then spread the remaining frosting over the top and sides of the cake. Sprinkle the remaining peanuts evenly over the top.

Serve at room temperature. Stored in an airtight container in the refrigerator, the cake will keep for about 1 week.

The Icing on the Cake

Cakes are very meaningful things. We need them for birthdays, anniversaries, and other celebrations, and we miss them terribly when they are not there. The vegan cakes in this book are all moist, hearty masterpieces of whole-wheat baking. The biggest challenge can be the frosting. Since frosting is typically made from white sugar and butter, margarine, or shortening, we vegans have to make a few detours to get to a sexy topper or glaze for our cakes, but I think you'll find that the recipes here offer elegant solutions.

Check out the Cashew Frosting on the stout cupcakes (page 184), which showcases vegan adaptation at its wholesome best. Naturally creamy raw cashews are puréed with a little natural sweetener, and—voilà!—a creamy frosting that can be piped and swirled for definite curb appeal. Likewise, vegan ganache need not be a contradiction in terms, as you'll discover when you try the version that tops the Pistachio Brownies (page 162). Tofu, a vegan baker's protein-packed secret ingredient, makes for a fabulous creamy frosting when puréed with chocolate, or even peanut butter, as in the Chocolate Layer Cake with Peanut Butter Frosting (page 176). With a little ingenuity, coconut milk, fruit purées, and a variety of whole foods can be transformed into fabulous toppings and glazes.

When it comes to cakes for special occasions, my favorite way to gussy them up with a gorgeous natural touch is to decorate them with fresh edible flowers. Just press the petals into the frosting and serve a cake dressed in blossoms. Of course, you can always use dried and fresh fruits in the same way.

Sweet Potato and Coconut Cupcakes with Coconut Frosting

Orange sweet potato gives these cupcakes a moist, lush texture that could be mistakenly attributed to dairy products. Roast a few sweet potatoes and purée what you need for this recipe; any leftovers make a great meal or snack. For a slightly different flavor, you could substitute pumpkin purée. The creamy frosting kicks up the curb appeal with not a bit of white sugar in sight.

Makes 12 cupcakes

INGREDIENTS

Frosting

One 13.5-oz/400-ml can coconut milk, chilled

½ cup/100 g palm sugar paste (see Tip, page 50), granular palm sugar, or Sucanat

3 tbsp arrowroot starch or cornstarch

1 tsp vanilla extract

¼ cup/65 g sweet potato purée

6 tbsp/35 g unsweetened shredded dried coconut, toasted (see Tip, page 181)

METHOD

To make the frosting: Turn the can of chilled coconut milk upside down and open the can. Pour off the liquid, reserving 3 tbsp. (Set aside the rest for another use.) Scrape out the solid coconut cream from the can; you should have about 1 cup.

In a small saucepan, combine the coconut cream and sugar. Bring to a boil over medium heat. Lower the heat and simmer, whisking constantly, until the sugar dissolves. In a cup or small bowl, whisk the reserved 3 tbsp coconut milk, arrowroot starch, and vanilla together to form a slurry. Pour into the saucepan and whisk until thoroughly blended. Cook, whisking often, until thickened, about 1 minute. Whisk in the sweet potato purée and toasted coconut. Transfer to a storage container and refrigerate for about 3 hours, until completely chilled.

Continued

Cupcakes

1½ cups/195 g whole-wheat pastry flour

½ cup/45 g unsweetened shredded dried coconut, plus 2 tbsp, toasted (see Tip)

1 tsp baking powder

1 tsp baking soda

½ tsp salt

¾ cup/150 g Sucanat or granular palm sugar

½ cup/120 ml coconut oil, melted

1 cup/245 g sweet potato purée

¾ cup/180 ml coconut milk or nondairy creamer

2 tbsp arrowroot starch or cornstarch

To make the cupcakes: Preheat the oven to 350°F/180°C/gas 4. Line twelve muffin cups with paper liners, then lightly oil the top of the pan so the cupcake tops don't stick.

In a large bowl, combine the flour, ½ cup/45 g coconut, baking powder, baking soda, and salt and whisk until well mixed. In a medium bowl, combine the Sucanat and coconut oil and stir until well mixed. Stir in the sweet potato purée. In a cup or small bowl, whisk the coconut milk and arrowroot starch together to form a slurry. Stir into the sweet potato mixture. Pour into the flour mixture and stir until well mixed.

Scoop the batter into the prepared muffin cups, dividing it evenly among them and using about a heaping ¼ cup/60 ml of batter per cupcake. Bake for 40 to 50 minutes, until a toothpick inserted in the center of a cupcake comes out clean and dry.

Transfer the pan to a wire rack and let cool completely. Turn out the cupcakes and spread rounded 2 tbsp of frosting over the top of each, then sprinkle with the 2 tbsp toasted coconut. Stored in an airtight container in the refrigerator, the cupcakes will keep for about 1 week.

TIP To toast dried coconut, preheat the oven to 300°F/150°C/gas 1. Spread the coconut on a rimmed baking sheet and bake until golden, about 8 minutes, stirring after about 5 minutes of baking.

Olive Oil Cupcakes with Hazelnuts and Gianduja Cream

In these cupcakes the olive oil is up front and center, allowing you to play with its flavors; you may enjoy a fruity oil, a peppery one, or one that's buttery and mild. The frosting is a vegan version of hazelnut-chocolate spread, without refined sugar and milk.

Makes 12 Cupcakes

INGREDIENTS

Gianduja Cream

¾ cup/90 g hazelnuts, toasted and skinned (see Tip, page 63)

½ cup/120 ml agave syrup

¼ cup/20 g Dutch-process cocoa powder

½ tsp vanilla extract

Cupcakes

1½ cups/195 g whole-wheat pastry flour

1 cup/115 g unbleached all-purpose flour

1 tsp baking powder

1 tsp baking soda

½ tsp salt

¾ cup/180 ml agave syrup

¾ cup/180 ml hazelnut milk or other nondairy milk

6 tbsp/90 ml extra-virgin olive oil

2 tsp apple cider vinegar

½ cup/60 g hazelnuts, toasted and skinned (see Tip, page 63) and coarsely chopped

METHOD

To make the cream: Put the hazelnuts in a blender or food processor and process until they form a paste and are smooth as possible. Add the agave syrup, cocoa powder, and vanilla and process until smooth. Refrigerate for at least 2 hours, until well chilled.

To make the cupcakes: Preheat the oven to 350°F/180°C/gas 4. Line twelve muffin cups with paper liners, then lightly oil the top of the pan so the cupcakes don't stick.

In a large bowl, combine both flours, the baking powder, baking soda, and salt and whisk until well mixed. In a medium bowl, combine the agave syrup, hazelnut milk, olive oil, and vinegar and whisk until thoroughly blended. Pour into the flour mixture and stir until just combined. Fold in the hazelnuts.

Scoop the batter into the prepared muffin cups, dividing it evenly among them; they should be full. Bake for 20 to 25 minutes, until the tops are deep golden and a toothpick inserted in the center of a cupcake comes out clean and dry.

Transfer the pan to a wire rack and let cool completely. Turn out the cupcakes and spread about 2 tbsp of cream over the top of each. Stored in an airtight container in the refrigerator, the cupcakes will keep for about 1 week.

Stout Cupcakes with Cashew Frosting

Deep, dark stout beer adds a pleasing bitterness to these cupcakes, while also giving them a little lift. Some beer makers use isinglass, which comes from fish, to strain sediment from their products, but others don't, so check to be sure the stout you purchase is vegan. A good source for information on vegan alcoholic beverages is Barnivore.com. Note that the cashews for the frosting should be soaked in advance, so plan ahead.

Makes 12 cupcakes

INGREDIENTS

Cashew Frosting

1 cup/115 g raw cashews, soaked for at least 2 hours

1 tbsp nutritional yeast (optional)

½ cup/120 ml nondairy creamer

½ cup/120 ml agave syrup

2 tbsp coconut oil, melted

3 tbsp arrowroot starch or cornstarch

½ tsp apple cider vinegar

½ tsp vanilla extract

Pinch of salt

METHOD

To make the frosting: Drain the cashews and put them in a blender. Blend on low speed until chopped, then add the nutritional yeast (if using). In a small saucepan, combine the nondairy creamer, agave syrup, coconut oil, arrowroot starch, vinegar, vanilla, and salt and whisk until smooth and thoroughly combined. Bring to a boil over medium heat and cook, whisking occasionally, until thickened, 3 to 5 minutes. Scrape the mixture into the blender and process until completely smooth, stopping to scrape down the sides a few times. Transfer to a storage container and refrigerate for at least 3 hours, until completely chilled.

Cupcakes

1 cup/130 g whole-wheat pastry flour

½ cup/60 g unbleached all-purpose flour

1 cup/200 g Sucanat or granular palm sugar

¼ cup/20 g Dutch-process cocoa powder

1 tsp baking soda

½ tsp baking powder

½ tsp salt

½ cup/120 ml nondairy milk

2 tbsp ground flaxseeds

1 tsp egg replacer, such as Ener-G

⅓ cup/75 ml coconut oil, melted

1 tsp vanilla extract

½ cup/120 ml stout beer

To make the cupcakes: Preheat the oven to 350°F/180°C/gas 4. Line twelve muffin cups with paper liners, then lightly oil the top of the pan so the cupcake tops don't stick.

In a large bowl, combine both flours, the sugar, cocoa powder, baking soda, baking powder, and salt and whisk until well mixed. In a medium bowl, whisk the nondairy milk, flaxseeds, and egg replacer together until smooth and frothy. Whisk in the coconut oil and vanilla. Pour into the flour mixture and stir until thoroughly combined; the mixture will be thick, so you may need to knead it by hand a bit. Add the beer and stir vigorously until well combined.

Scoop the batter into the prepared muffin cups, dividing it evenly among them and using about a scant ¼ cup/60 ml of batter per cupcake. Bake for 25 minutes, until a toothpick inserted in the center of a cupcake comes out clean and dry.

Transfer the pan to a wire rack and let cool completely. Turn out the cupcakes and spread about 2 tbsp of frosting over the top of each, or for a more decorative presentation, use a pastry bag to pipe the frosting over the cupcakes. Stored in an airtight container in the refrigerator, the cupcakes will keep for about 1 week.

Chocolate-Cherry Cupcakes with Chocolate Frosting

Cherries and chocolate are a perfect combination, and here they conspire to conceal the healthful squash purée lurking in these delicious cupcakes. The frosting is a classic tofu pudding, and you may want to make a double batch so you'll have plenty left to snack on!

Makes 12 cupcakes

INGREDIENTS

Frosting

6 oz/170 g silken tofu, drained and pressed (see Tip, page 188)

½ cup/120 ml brown rice syrup

½ cup/85 g vegan chocolate chips

Cupcakes

½ cup/120 ml nondairy milk

1 tbsp ground flaxseeds

¼ cup/60 ml vegetable oil

¼ cup/20 g Dutch process cocoa powder

¾ cup/185 g winter squash purée (see Tip, page 93)

¾ cup/100 g whole-wheat pastry flour

½ cup/60 g unbleached flour

1 cup/200 g granular palm sugar, palm sugar paste (see Tip, page 50), or Sucanat

¾ tsp baking soda

¼ tsp salt

¼ tsp ground nutmeg

½ cup/85 g dried cherries

METHOD

To make the frosting: In a blender or food processor, purée the tofu. Scrape down the sides and process again until completely smooth. Add the brown rice syrup and process until thoroughly blended.

Melt the chocolate chips in a double boiler or a microwave (see Tip, page 105), then scrape the chips into the tofu mixture. Process immediately, before the chocolate hardens, until smooth and well blended, stopping to scrape down the sides a few times. Transfer to a storage container and refrigerate until completely chilled, at least 4 hours.

To make the cupcakes: Preheat the oven to 350°F/180°C/gas 4. Lightly oil twelve muffin cups or line them with paper liners, then lightly oil the top of the pan so the cupcake tops don't stick.

In a cup or small bowl, whisk the nondairy milk and flaxseeds together and let stand for 5 minutes.

In medium bowl, stir the vegetable oil and cocoa powder together until thoroughly blended. Stir in the squash purée and the flaxseed mixture. In a large bowl, combine both flours, the sugar, baking soda, salt, and nutmeg. Add the cocoa mixture and gently stir until just combined. Fold in the cherries.

Continued

Scoop the batter into the prepared muffin cups, dividing it evenly among them; they should be about two-thirds full. Bake for 20 minutes, until a toothpick inserted in the center of a cupcake comes out with moist crumbs attached.

Transfer the pan to a wire rack and let cool completely. Turn out the cupcakes and spread about 2 tbsp of frosting over the top of each. Stored in an airtight container in the refrigerator, the cupcakes will keep for about 1 week.

TIP The tofu in the frosting must be pressed to remove excess liquid and achieve optimum results. Wrap the tofu tightly in a clean kitchen towel and place on a cutting board, then place a baking pan or pot on top, then put a can or other weight on top to press down on the tofu. Since this is silken tofu, a heavy weight might crush it, so don't press too hard. Press for at least 20 minutes. Since you are puréeing it, it is okay if it breaks a little.

Mini Fruitcakes with Rum Glaze

There's no law that says that fruitcakes have to be terrible. In fact, if you make them with unsweetened dried fruit and other high-quality ingredients, they can be downright wonderful—and good for you, too. As the saying goes, good things come to those who wait, and you will have to be patient with this recipe. First, the dried fruit must soak for at least a day. Then, to really drench the cakes, the rum glaze that takes these mini fruitcakes over the top should be basted over the cakes a few times over the course of several days—or weeks. It may be hard to wait, but you'll be glad you did.

Makes 9 mini fruitcakes

INGREDIENTS

4 oz/115 g chopped dried mango

1 cup/170 g dried cherries

1 cup/170 g dried apricots

¾ cup/180 ml dark rum

1¾ cups/230 g whole-wheat pastry flour

½ tsp baking powder

¼ tsp salt

1 tsp ground cinnamon

½ tsp ground allspice

⅛ tsp ground nutmeg

⅛ tsp ground cloves

½ cup/120 ml nondairy milk

2 tbsp egg replacer, such as Ener-G

¾ cup/180 ml agave syrup

½ cup/120 ml coconut oil, melted

½ tsp vanilla extract

Rum Glaze

½ cup/120 ml dark rum

½ cup/120 ml agave syrup

METHOD

In a medium saucepan, combine all the dried fruits and the rum. Bring to a simmer over medium heat, then cover and remove from the heat. Let stand for 30 minutes. Transfer to a storage container, cover, and refrigerate for at least 24 hours and up to 3 days.

Preheat the oven to 350°F/180°C/gas 4. Oil nine muffin cups.

In a large bowl, combine the flour, baking powder, salt, cinnamon, allspice, nutmeg, and cloves and whisk until well mixed. In a medium bowl, whisk the nondairy milk and egg replacer together until smooth and frothy. Add the agave syrup, coconut oil, and vanilla and whisk until well blended. Pour into the flour mixture and stir until well combined. Fold in the soaked fruit. (Reserve any leftover soaking liquid for the glaze.)

Scoop the batter into the prepared muffin cups, dividing it evenly among them; they should be full. Bake for 30 minutes, until the tops are golden and a toothpick inserted in the center of a cake comes out clean and dry. Transfer the pan to a wire rack and let cool completely.

To make the glaze: Whisk the rum and agave syrup together until thoroughly combined.

Put the cakes in a storage container and baste with the glaze to coat, reserving the remaining glaze to baste them daily as long as they last. (If you run out of glaze, you can make more and just keep going.) Refrigerate, tightly covered. Try to let the cakes soak up the glaze for at least 1 day before serving.

Serve at room temperature. Stored in an airtight container in the refrigerator, the cakes will keep for about 3 weeks.

Coconut Shortcakes with Bananas and Coconut Cream

These melt-in-your-mouth treats are proof that vegans need not do without tender shortcakes with fruit and a whipped, creamy topping. Make sure to chill the coconut cream mixture thoroughly and keep it cold so that it will hold some air when you whip it. You can try this recipe with whatever fruit is in season, from mango to strawberries.

Serves 10

INGREDIENTS

Whipped Coconut Cream

Two 13.5-oz/400-ml cans coconut milk, chilled

½ cup/100 g palm sugar paste (see Tip, page 50), granular palm sugar, or Sucanat

METHOD

To make the whipped coconut cream: Turn the cans of chilled coconut milk upside down and open the cans. Pour off the liquid and reserve it for another use. Scrape the solid coconut cream into a small saucepan. Add the sugar and bring to a simmer over low heat. Cook, whisking constantly, until the sugar dissolves. Let cool briefly, then cover and refrigerate until completely chilled, about 3 hours or overnight. Put a mixing bowl and the beaters of an electric mixer in the freezer. It's best to whip the mixture just before serving the shortcakes.

Preheat the oven to 400°F/200°C/gas 6. Line a baking sheet with parchment paper.

To make the shortcakes: In a large bowl, combine both flours, ¼ cup/ 25 g untoasted coconut, the baking powder, baking soda, and salt and whisk until well mixed. Grate the chilled coconut oil into the flour mixture, then toss until the bits of coconut oil are evenly coated. Mix gently with your fingers, squeezing to break up the bits and working quickly so the warmth from your hands doesn't melt the coconut oil.

In a small bowl, combine the mashed banana, agave syrup, coconut milk, vanilla, and coconut extract and whisk until thoroughly blended. Pour into the flour mixture and stir until just combined.

Shortcakes

1 cup/130 g whole-wheat pastry flour

½ cup/60 g unbleached all-purpose flour

¼ cup/25 g unsweetened shredded dried coconut, plus ¼ cup/25 g, toasted (see Tip, page 181)

2 tsp baking powder

½ tsp baking soda

½ tsp salt

½ cup/120 ml coconut oil, chilled (see Tip, page 129)

½ cup/120 ml mashed banana, plus 5 medium bananas, sliced

½ cup/120 ml agave syrup

¼ cup/60 ml coconut milk

½ tsp vanilla extract

¼ tsp coconut or almond extract

2 tbsp nondairy milk

2 tsp fresh lemon juice

Scrape the dough out onto a floured work surface and pat it to a thickness of about ¾ in/2 cm. Cut with a 3-in/7.5-cm biscuit cutter. Gently pat the scraps together and cut again. You should have about 10 shortcakes. Brush the tops with the nondairy milk. Sprinkle the toasted coconut evenly over the tops and press it in gently so it adheres.

Use a metal spatula to transfer the shortcakes to the lined baking sheet. Bake for 15 minutes, until golden on top and browned on the underside.

Meanwhile, put the sliced bananas in a medium bowl. Sprinkle with the lemon juice and stir gently until evenly coated.

Working quickly, remove the chilled coconut cream mixture from the refrigerator and the bowl and beaters from the freezer. Transfer the coconut cream mixture to the bowl and beat on high speed for about 4 minutes, until fluffy.

Cool the shortcakes for 5 minutes on the pan. While still warm, split them and put about one-tenth of the bananas and ¼ cup/60 ml of the whipped coconut cream between the layers. Serve right away.

The shortcakes can be stored in an airtight container in the refrigerator for up to 1 week. If you are only serving a few at a time, only whip enough cream and slice enough bananas for that amount, as neither stores well.

Cornmeal Shortcakes with Strawberries and Vanilla Ice Cream

In this recipe, the combo of sunny yellow cornmeal and sweet red strawberries comes together under a creamy scoop of vegan ice cream. After you've made the ice cream for this dessert once, you'll want to keep some around for those times when the inevitable ice-cream craving hits.

Serves 9

INGREDIENTS

1 cup/130 g whole-wheat pastry flour

½ cup/60 g masa flour or corn flour (see Tip)

½ cup/80 g cornmeal

½ cup/100 g Sucanat or granular palm sugar

2 tsp baking powder

½ tsp baking soda

½ tsp salt

½ cup/120 ml coconut oil, chilled (see Tip, page 129)

½ cup/120 ml nondairy creamer

½ tsp vanilla extract

1½ lb/680 g fresh strawberries, sliced

½ cup/120 ml agave syrup

2½ cups vegan Vanilla Ice Cream (page 194) or store-bought

METHOD

Preheat the oven to 400°F/200°C/gas 6.

In a large bowl, combine the pastry flour, masa flour, cornmeal, Sucanat, baking powder, baking soda, and salt and whisk until well mixed. Grate the chilled coconut oil into the flour mixture, then toss until the bits of coconut oil are evenly coated. Mix gently with your fingers, squeezing to break up the bits and working quickly so the warmth from your hands doesn't melt the coconut oil.

In a cup or small bowl, whisk the nondairy creamer and vanilla together. Pour into the flour mixture and stir until just combined.

Scrape the dough out onto a floured work surface and shape it into a 7-in/17-cm square about ¾ in/2 cm thick. Cut 3 by 3, to make 9 squares.

Transfer the shortcakes to an ungreased baking sheet. Bake for 15 minutes, until golden on top and browned on the underside.

Meanwhile, in a medium saucepan combine the strawberries and agave syrup. Bring to a boil over medium heat. Lower the heat and simmer, stirring occasionally, until the strawberries are soft and the syrup is thickened, about 10 minutes.

Cool the shortcakes on the pan for 5 minutes. Serve warm or at room temperature, topping each with about ⅛ cup/75 ml strawberries and ¼ cup/60 ml ice cream. Stored in separate airtight containers in the refrigerator, the shortcakes and strawberries will keep for about 1 week.

TIP U.K. readers take note—Corn flour is made from maize, not to be confused with the white, powdered corn flour used as a starch.

Vanilla Ice Cream

Vanilla ice cream, in a vegan book? Of course, with coconut milk or rich nondairy creamers, it's as easy as it is delicious. This is a wonderful recipe to use traditional palm sugar paste in, since it gets dissolved in the milk before chilling, giving the ice cream a luscious, caramel flavor. Make this to accompany the dessert recipes in this book, or just for enjoying on its own. It's that good.

Makes 2½ cups/600 ml

INGREDIENTS

½ cup/120 ml nondairy milk

½ cup/100 g palm sugar paste (see Tip, page 50), or ½ cup/120 ml agave syrup

2 cups/480 ml coconut milk or nondairy creamer

1 tbsp arrowroot starch or cornstarch

1 tsp vanilla extract

METHOD

In a small saucepan, combine the nondairy milk and sugar. Cook, stirring constantly, over low heat until the sugar dissolves. In a cup or small bowl, whisk 2 tbsp of the coconut milk and the arrowroot starch together to form a slurry. Pour the slurry into the saucepan and whisk until thoroughly combined. Cook, whisking constantly, until the mixture comes to a boil. Remove from the heat and whisk in the vanilla and remaining coconut milk.

Refrigerate until completely chilled, then freeze in an ice-cream maker according to the manufacturer's instructions. Stored in the freezer, the ice cream will keep for about 1 month.

Phyllo Sticks Filled with Cashew-Chocolate Crunch

Break away from the standard cookie and make these alluring little finger foods. They are a great way to finish off those extra sheets of phyllo left over after making Miniature Caramel-Apple Tarts (page 143) or Three-Nut Baklava (page 197). These crunchy, golden brown treats filled with nuts, chocolate, and raisins are so tasty that no one will suspect that they are whole-wheat or vegan. The only question you're likely to hear is "Do you have any more?"

Makes 18 phyllo sticks

INGREDIENTS

¼ cup/40 g vegan chocolate chips

¼ cup/30 g cashews, toasted (see Tip, page 59) and chopped

¼ cup/40 g raisins

2 tsp agave syrup

3 sheets whole-wheat phyllo dough, thawed overnight in the refrigerator

3 tbsp olive oil, mild to medium in flavor

METHOD

Preheat the oven to 400°F/200°C/gas 6. Line a baking sheet with parchment paper, then oil the paper.

Chop the chocolate chips with a sharp knife or by pulsing briefly in a food processor. Transfer to a small bowl. Add the cashews and raisins, drizzle with the agave syrup, and stir until thoroughly combined.

Place one sheet of the phyllo on the counter and brush it with some of the olive oil. Cut the sheet into six rectangles. Place a scant 1 tbsp of the chocolate mixture on each rectangle in a line down the middle, leaving a ¾-in/2-cm border at each end. Fold the short ends over the filling, then roll from one long side to make a cigarette shape. Place the rolls on the prepared pan and brush with olive oil. Repeat with the remaining ingredients.

Bake for 15 to 20 minutes, until the phyllo is golden and crisp. Transfer the pan to a wire rack to cool for 10 minutes, then transfer the pastries to the rack and let cool completely. Stored in an airtight container at room temperature, the phyllo sticks will keep for about 1 week.

Three-Nut Baklava

Baklava is a perfect candidate for veganization. The classic pastry is usually made with butter, a copious amount of syrup made with white sugar and honey, and phyllo dough made with white flour. This version is lighter and less syrupy sweet, creating a healthful, nutty dessert that everyone can feel good about enjoying.

Makes 36 pieces

INGREDIENTS

½ cup/100 g Sucanat

½ tsp ground cinnamon

1 cup/115 g walnuts

1 cup/115 g pistachios

¾ cup/115 g almonds

12 sheets whole-wheat phyllo dough, thawed overnight in the refrigerator

½ cup/120 ml light olive oil or melted coconut oil

1 cup/240 ml agave syrup

½ cup/120 ml water

Zest from 1 large lemon, removed in one long strip

METHOD

Preheat the oven to 350°F/180°C/gas 4. Oil a 13-by-9-in/33-by-23-cm baking pan.

In a blender, combine the Sucanat and cinnamon and grind until powdery. Transfer to a small bowl.

In the blender or a food processor, pulse the walnuts until minced but still a bit chunky. Transfer to a small bowl and stir in one-third of the Sucanat mixture. Do the same for the pistachios and the almonds.

Cover the phyllo sheets with a large piece of plastic wrap, then cover that with a barely damp towel. Remove one sheet and brush half of it with olive oil. Fold the sheet in half and place it in the prepared pan, then brush the top with olive oil. Repeat with two more sheets. Spread the walnuts over the top in an even layer. Repeat the layering with three more sheets of phyllo, an even layer of the pistachios, three more sheets of phyllo, and an even layer of the almonds. Layer the last three sheets of phyllo over the top.

Using a sharp paring knife, score the pastry across the 9-in/23-cm length of the pan to form six strips. Next, cut corner to corner, and then cut parallel to that slice two times on each side. Bake for 40 minutes, until the phyllo is lightly golden and crisp.

In a small saucepan, combine the agave syrup, water, and lemon zest. Bring to a boil over high heat, then lower the heat and simmer, stirring occasionally, for 10 minutes. Let cool slightly, then remove the zest.

Pour the syrup over the pastry. Cover the baklava and refrigerate for at least 1 hour before serving. Stored in the refrigerator, tightly covered, the baklava will keep for about 2 weeks.

RESOURCES

Flours, arrowroot starch, oats, and many other foods:
Bob's Red Mill
BobsRedMill.com
5000 SE International Way
Milwaukie, OR 97222
800-553-2258

Ener-G Egg Replacer:
Ener-G Foods
Ener-G.com
5960 1st Avenue S
Seattle, WA 98108
800-331-5222

Flaxseeds:
North American Nutrition
GoldenFlax.com
PO Box 456
Warroad, MN 56763
800-387-5516

Agave syrup:
Better Body Foods & Nutrition
Xagave.com
1762 West 20 South, Unit #5
Lindon, UT 84042
866-404-6582

Dry-form palm sugar:
BigTreeFarms.com
541-488-5605

Wet-form palm sugar:
Amazon.com/Thai-Palm-Sugar-16-package/dp/B000EUD8M8

Sucanat:
Wholesome Sweeteners
WholesomeSweeteners.com
8016 Highway 90-A
Sugar Land, TX 77478
800-680-1896

INDEX